Praise for
Women's Quotations for Successful Living

"Powerful women are inspiration. *Women's Quotations for Successful Living* will inspire, encourage, and motivate you to go after your dreams."

Jennifer Broome

Television Host, Meteorologist,
Travel Expert, and Adventurer

"I've always looked up to confident women. This collection makes it easy to find inspiration any day of the week."

Julia Mancuso

American World Cup Alpine Ski Racer
and Olympic Gold Medalist

"Everyone needs a little inspiration. Caroline, Sarah, and Hal have gathered a collection of quotes to keep you going every day."

Robin Schepper

Former Executive Director, Let's Move Initiative
Office of the First Lady of the United States

Women's Quotations for Successful Living

edited by
ıan. – First

rom seven
rld leaders,
explorers,
– Provided

armichael,

Quotations

r

l Living

d Edited by

lan Levin
e Carmichael
oleman

oks, Inc.
York

This edition published by SelectBooks, Inc.
For information address SelectBooks, Inc., New York,

First Edition

ISBN 978-1-59079-268-1

Cataloging-in-Publication Data

Library of Congress Cataloging-in-Publication Data
Women's quotations for successful living / compiled an
Howard Alan Levin, Caroline Lalive Carmichael, Sarah Cole
edition.

    pages cm
Includes index.
Summary: "Compilation of eleven hundred quotations
hundred well-known and accomplished women, including w
Olympians, physicians, athletes, actors, artists, executives
adventurers, and authors. Sources of all quotations are cited
by publisher.
    ISBN 978-1-59079-268-1 (pbk. : alk. paper)
    1. Women–Quotations. I. Levin, Howard Alan. II.
Caroline Lalive. III. Coleman, Sarah,
    1978-
PN6081.5.W5848 2014
082'.082–dc23

                    2014012150

Manufactured in the United States of Americ
            10 9 8 7 6 5 4 3 2 1

Dedicated to your extraordinary life

Contents

Introduction

Coauthors, friends, and business partners Howard Alan Levin
(Hal), Caroline Lalive Carmichael, and Sarah Coleman share
a love and passion for helping people. Each has found his and
her own way to inspire individuals through coaching, training,
healing, and motivating others to live fuller, happier, and more
meaningful lives.

Together they started a new company, *Inspired Life Net-*
work, to create a unique opportunity for women who are seeking to form their own extraordinary lives through workshops,
seminars, and ultimately becoming a part of a larger network
of supporters.

The authors discovered early on in their friendship that
throughout their lives each has found inspiration and encouragement from meaningful quotations. Hal's first book, *Quota-*
tions for Successful Living: How to Live Life, is a chronological
collection of quotes from great thinkers and inspiring leaders
spanning more than four millennia. When they came together
to create *Inspired Life Network*, based on the premise of women
mentoring and inspiring other women, the idea of *Women's*
Quotations for Successful Living was naturally conceived.

After reviewing tens of thousands of quotes, they selected
the most uplifting. Their collection includes thought-provoking
and inspirational messages from more than six hundred successful women, including world leaders, Olympians, physicians,

athletes, actors, artists, executives, explorers, adventurers, and authors. Goddesses, all!

Every quote includes its source, enabling the reader to easily search the quote to gather a deeper meaning within the context of the passage. The sources of the quotations include books, interviews, speeches, magazines, newspapers, and television programs, among others.

HAL LEVIN, an entrepreneur, professional spiritual healer, and world traveler, has a vision. He has met women all over the world, from impoverished mothers to world leaders. One commonality he's found among all women is their desire to achieve more in their lives and to live with more passion.

While observing the gender inequality in nearly all societies and populations, he has seen the urgent need for more female leaders. He believes a dedication to the goal of increasing female mentors and role models can bring our world into a better balance. It's a tall order, but Hal wants to do what he can to evoke that change.

Two of Hal's favorite quotes from the book are:

Literature is my utopia.

Helen Keller

Realizing the obstacles that Helen overcame helps to diminish Hal's own obstacles.

Time wounds all heels.

Jane Ace

This quote reminds Hal to let go of transgressors and let karma take care of things.

CAROLINE LALIVE CARMICHAEL, an Olympian (Nagano 1998 and Salt Lake City 2002) and three-time United States National Alpine Skiing Champion, spent thirteen years on the U.S. Ski team. Caroline now works as a television sports commentator, professional fundraiser, model, and ski coach. She knows how goal-setting, hard work, perseverance, dedication, and the support of community can lead to success and fulfillment. Articulate, passionate and funny, Caroline has the compassion, confidence, and skills to inspire others by sharing her experiences beyond the ski slope.

Caroline states, "I believe that life is what you make it, and while I experience a good life, I still often find myself focusing on what I haven't achieved. The following quotes are favorites of mine because they remind me that life is about loving others and daring to dream":

Life should not be measured by the awards we receive, but rather by the rewards we enjoy knowing how many lives we have empowered.

June Wolff, MD and mentor to Caroline.

Go confidently in the direction of your dreams!
Live the life you've imagined.

Henry David Thoreau

SARAH COLEMAN has always enjoyed an outdoor lifestyle and many sports from skiing to biking. Her love of sports and fitness and a degree in communications motivated Sarah to start two companies dedicated to living healthy lifestyles: *A Weight Lifted Fitness Camp* and *Food To Fit* nutrition packages. Sarah understands that to live a balanced and inspired life, one must start with the basics of healthy fitness and nutritional habits. Sarah's creativity shines and her positive outlook is contagious.

Two of Sarah's favorite quotes are:

Be a rainbow in someone else's cloud.

Maya Angelou

This quote makes Sarah smile, and she knows that you can always make someone else's day better no matter what battle you are fighting.

Adventure is worthwhile in itself.

Amelia Earhart

This sparks imagination while captivating the adventurous spirit. Sarah uses these quotes to inspire herself, motivate her fitness clients, and friends.

Hal, Caroline, and Sarah sincerely hope you enjoy and profit from the incredible women represented in *Women's Quotations for Successful Living*. These women dare to push forward, to live inspiring and extraordinary lives and to make this world a better place.

This book is dedicated to them and you!

If you have an inspiring quote, please share it at: www.InspiredLifeNetwork.com

Time wounds all heels.

Easy Aces, American radio comedy show

Jane Ace

ॐ

I can hear of the brilliant accomplishments of any of my sex with pleasure and rejoice in that liberality of sentiment which acknowledges them.

Letter to John Adams

Abigail Adams

ॐ

Civilization is a method of living, an attitude of equal respect for all men.

Essays and Speeches on Peace

Nothing could be worse than the fear that one had given up too soon, and left one unexpended effort that might have saved the world.

The Search for Negotiated Peace:
Women's Activism and Citizen Diplomacy in World War I

Jane Addams

ॐ

The Rubicons which women must cross, the sex barriers which they must breach, are ultimately those that exist in their own minds.

Sisters in Crime

Freda Adler

People take sex far too seriously.

Newsweek magazine

The roughest road often leads to the top.

Official Twitter account

I think women are sensual, beautiful beings, and I feel empowered when I express myself sexually.

Glamour magazine

Christina Aguilera

ॐ

You can only perceive real beauty in a person as they get older.

The Guardian, U. K.

Anouk Aimee

ॐ

Young women should pave their own way. I find it quite confining to live up to anybody else's expectations of who you should be.

Marie Claire magazine

Jessica Alba

ॐ

It took me quite a long time to develop a voice, and now that I have it, I am not going to be silent.

Interview with Marianne Schnall

Madeleine Albright

Love is a great beautifier.

Little Women

I'm not afraid of storms, for I'm learning to sail my ship.

Letter to the American Woman Suffrage Association

Far away there in the sunshine are my highest aspirations. I cannot reach them: but I can look up and see their beauty, believe in them, and try to follow where they lead.

Work: A Story of Experience

Louisa May Alcott

༄

With every dollar you save a dime, you spend a quarter or fifty cents, and you give some of it away. To me, that's the spiritual use of money.

I Dream a World by Brian Lanker

Margaret Walker Alexander

༄

I think as long as you're not being malicious and you're not hurting people then you should not be ashamed of what you do.

GQ magazine

Lily Allen

༄

All you can do, every day, is to learn the truth as best you can.

Game of Patience

Susanne Alleyn

When people think of angels, they think flowing robes and halos. But in the Bible, they also look like ordinary people. Why Not today?

In the Arms of Angels

Joan Wester Anderson

૭

As long as you keep a person down, some part of you has to be down there to hold him down, so it means you cannot soar as you might otherwise.

Magnificent Women in Music by Heather Ball

Marian Anderson

૭

Eventually you just have to realize that you're living for an audience of one. I'm not here for anyone else's approval.

Esquire magazine

Pamela Anderson

૭

Be a rainbow in someone else's cloud.

Letter to My Daughter

If you find it in your heart to care for somebody else, you will have succeeded.

A Brave and Startling Truth

You may not control all the events that happen to you, but you can decide not to be reduced by them.

Letter to My Daughter

I've learned that people will forget what you said, people will forget what you did, but people will never forget how you made them feel.

MayaAngelou.com

Life is not measured by the number of breaths we take, but by the moments that take our breath away. You can't use up creativity. The more you use, the more you have.

Conversations with Maya Angelou by Jeffrey Eliot

Maya Angelou

ა

Relationships are two people; everyone is accountable. A lot goes into a relationship coming together, and a lot goes into a relationship falling apart. Even if it's 98 percent the other person's fault, it's 2 percent yours . . . You can only clean up your side of the street.

Vanity Fair magazine

Jennifer Aniston

ა

The Queens in history compare favorably with the Kings.

History of Women Suffrage, 1848–1861

Join the union, girls, and together say, "Equal pay for equal work."

History of Women Suffrage, 1848–1861

Woman must not depend upon the protection of man, but must be taught to protect herself.

History of Women Suffrage, 1848–1861

I think the girl who is able to earn her own living and pay her own way should be as happy as anybody on earth. The sense of independence and security is very sweet.

The Life and Work of Susan B. Anthony
by Ida Husted Harper

Susan B. Anthony

ͽ

I am not embarrassed to tell you that I believe in miracles.

Borrowed Narratives by Harold Ivan Smith

Corazon Aquino

ͽ

Love involves a peculiar unfathomable combination of understanding and misunderstanding.

The Biography Channel

Diane Arbus

ͽ

Everyone wants to be appreciated, so if you appreciate someone, don't keep it a secret.

Mary Kay, *You Can Have It All*

If today one more woman learns how great she really is, then for me it has been a great day.

Miracles Happen

Don't limit yourself. Many people limit themselves to what they think they can do. You can go as far as your mind lets you. What you believe, remember, you can achieve.

Entrepreneurship Management by Bholanath Dutta

Mary Kay Ash

૭

In passing, also, I would like to say that the first time Adam had a chance he laid the blame on woman.

My Two Countries

Nancy Astor

૭

Some people only care about themselves. They use things; they destroy things. You're a creator, a builder. A healer, not a user.

Midnight Predator

Amelia Atwater-Rhodes

૭

It is better to hope than to mope!

The Year of the Flood

The Eskimo has fifty-two names for snow because it is important to them; there ought to be as many for love.

Surfacing

Margaret Atwood

We have all a better guide in ourselves. if we would attend to it, than any other person can be.

Mansfield Park

Why not seize the opportunity at once? How often is happiness destroyed by preparation, foolish preparation.

Emma

Friendship is certainly the finest balm for the pangs of disappointed love.

Northanger Abbey

Jane Austen

ھ

Imagination is the highest kite one can fly.

Lauren Bacall By Myself

Being a liberal is the best thing on earth you can be.

Larry King Live

Lauren Bacall

ھ

I took a gamble, to exercise leadership without losing my feminine nature.

The New York Times

I know from my own experience that there is no limit to what women can do.

Speech launching UN Women

The biggest challenges everywhere are political participation and economic empowerment—and ending violence against women.

The New York Times

Michelle Bachelet

ဢ

You don't get to choose how you're going to die, or when. You can only decide how you're going to live. Now!

Daybreak

Joan Baez

ဢ

You never find yourself until you face the truth.

The Raw Pearl

Pearl Bailey

ဢ

All my life, the naysayers have told me that I can't win because I'm a progressive . . . because I'm a woman . . . even because I'm a lesbian. And I've proven them wrong.

Ms. magazine

You know, what I would say in terms of crashing through the glass ceiling is, you know, if you're not in the room the conversation is about you. If you're in the room, the conversation is with you. That does transform things.

Interview by Kevin Cirilli

Tammy Baldwin

I have an everyday religion that works for me: Love yourself first and everything else falls into line. You really have to love yourself to get anything done in this world.

The Connection by Anthony Silard

It's a helluva start, being able to recognize what makes you happy.

The Lucy Book of Lists by Michael Karol

The secret of staying young is to live honestly, eat slowly, and just not think about your age.

Reader's Digest magazine

Lucille Ball

৯

Self-love has very little to with how you feel about your outer self. It's about accepting all of yourself/

Woman's Day magazine

Tyra Banks

৯

I don't think when I make love.

Sex and Intimacy

It is sad to grow old but nice to ripen.

Blueprints for High Availability

Brigitte Bardot

The idea of strictly mind your own business is moldy rubbish. Who could be so selfish?

Forbes magazine

Myrtie Barker

ை

Finding a calm place inside myself through meditation kind of helped me to get over a lot of mental illness . . . It's just been really great in my life.

Larry King Live

The thing women have yet to learn is that nobody gives you power, you just have to take it.

Women and Society by Rakesh Gupta

There's a lot more to being a woman than being a mother, but there's a hell of a lot more to being a mother than most people suspect.

The Children We Deserve by Rosalind Miles

Birth control that really works: Every night before we go to bed we spent an hour with our kids.

Woman to Woman by Julia Gilden and Mark Friedman.

Roseanne Barr

ை

My rules are your rules.

CNN Money

The most important thing we have to drive into the business every day is that it all starts and ends with great product.

Los Angeles Times

Problems don't go away when you ignore them—they get bigger. In my experience, it is much better to get the right people together, to make a plan, and to address every challenge head on.

Kettering University commencement speech

Mary Barra

The healthy and strong individual is the one who asks for help when he needs it. Whether he's got an abscess on his knee or in his soul.

Getting Out by Kathy Cawthon

Rona Barrett

You grow up the day you have the first real laugh at yourself.

Simple Retreats for a Woman's Soul by Sue Augustine

You must learn day by day, year by year to broaden your horizon. The more things you love, the more you are interested in, the more you enjoy, the more you are indignant about—the more you have left when anything happens.

The Barrymores by Hollis Alpert

Ethel Barrymore

Power can be seen as power with rather than power over, and it can be used for competence and co-operation, rather than dominance and control.

Blessings from the Fall by Beverly Engel

Anne L. Barstow

⚓

Love's language everywhere is known.

Love's Language

If we drink from the fountain of wisdom,
We thirst for its waters e'ermore.

Thoughts

Ardelia Cotton Barton

⚓

Everybody's business is nobody's business and nobody's business is my business.

Angel of the Battlefield by Ishbel Ross

Clara Barton

You don't get ulcers from what you eat. You get them from what's eating you.

The Subconscious Diet by Hugh B. Sanders

Vicki Baum

❧

See into life—don't just look at it.

Soul Beautiful, Naturally by Leanna Burns

I wasn't afraid to fail. Something good always comes out of failure.

Stepping Stones, edited by Jill Scevak

Ann Baxter

❧

Gratitude unlocks the fullness of life. It turns what we have into enough, and more.

The Language of Letting Go

Melody Beattie

❧

One is not born a woman, one becomes one.

The Second Sex

There is only one good. And that is to act according to the dictates of one's conscience.

All Men Are Mortal

Self-knowledge is no guarantee of happiness, but it is on the side of happiness and can supply the courage to fight for it.

Forces of Circumstances

We must not confuse the present with the past. With regard to the past, no further action is possible.

The Ethics of Ambiguity

One's life has value so long as one attributes value to the life of others, by means of love, friendship, indignation and compassion.

The Coming of Age

Simone de Beauvoir

෨

Your life follows your attention. Wherever you look, you end up going.

MarthaBeck.com

To attract something that you want, become as joyful as you think that thing would make you. The joy, not the thing, is the point.

O, The Oprah Magazine

Martha Beck

෨

With the power of conviction, there is no sacrifice,

Invincible

Pat Benatar

෨

Words are a form of action, capable of influencing change. Their articulation represents a complete, lived experience.

Losing Twice

Ingrid Bengis

As time passes we all get better at blazing a trail through the thicket of advice.

Farewell Crown and Goodbye King

Margot Bennett

৬

Above all, remember that the most important thing you can take anywhere is not a Gucci bag or French-cut jeans, it's an open mind.

MsAdventures by Gail Rubin Bereny

Gail Rubin Bereny

৬

Men say they love independence in a woman, but they don't waste a second demolishing it brick by brick.

Good Housekeeping magazine

Candice Bergen

৬

Happiness is good health and a bad memory.

The Biography Channel

I've never sought success in order to get fame and money; it's the talent and the passion that count in success.

Split Ends

Ingrid Bergman

You have a choice every moment of the day to open yourself up. And when you do that, it opens channels of love, joy, and especially sexual energy.

The Huffington Post

There's a yin and yang in relationships. It's about learning what nourishes your partner. Stop trying to love your partner the way you want to be loved and learn the way they want to be loved. Then share the way you want to be loved.

O, The Oprah Magazine

Laura Berman

ॐ

Love is the only shocking act left on the face of the earth.

Parted Lips

Sandra Bernhardt

ॐ

The time you need to do something is when no one else is willing to do it, when people are saying it can't be done.

American Social Thought

Mary Frances Berry

ॐ

One of the most courageous things you can do is identify yourself, know who you are, what you believe in and where you want to go.

Sheila

Murray Bethel

The most alluring thing a woman can have is confidence.

Cosmopolitan magazine, U.K.

I think it's healthy for a person to be nervous. It means you care.

Redbook magazine

We're all going through our problems, but we all have the same insecurities, and we all have the same abilities, and we all need each other.

The Biography Channel

Beyonce (Knowles)

∽

Character contributes to beauty.

Los Angeles Times

Ideally, couples need three lives; one for him, one for her, and one for them together.

Love Notebook by Running Press

Jacqueline Bisset

∽

The brain is not, and cannot be, the sole or complete organ of thought and feeling.

The Sexes Throughout Nature

Antoinette Brown Blackwell

∽

Events reveal people's characters; they don't determine them.

AmyBloom.com

It takes something to get married: nerve, hope, a strong desire to make a certain statement—and it takes something to stay married: more hope, determination, a sense of humor, and needs that are best met by being in a pair.

Live Your Best Life by Oprah Winfrey

Amy Bloom

♋

He alone is great Who by a life heroic conquers fate.

The Inevitable

Sarah Knowles Bolton

♋

If you can't make it better, you can laugh at it.

Time magazine

People are always asking couples whose marriage has endured at least a quarter of a century for their secret for success. Actually, it's no secret at all. I am a forgiving woman. Long ago, I forgave my husband for not being Paul Newman.

I Lost Everything in the Post-Natal Depression

Erma Bombeck

♋

Worry does not empty tomorrow of its sorrow, it empties today of its strength.

Values for Life

Corrie Boom

♋

I know what men want. Men want to be really, really close to someone who will leave them alone.

David Letterman Show

Elayne Boosler

A spiritually optimistic point of view holds that the universe is woven out of a fabric of love. Everything that happens is ultimately for the good if we're willing to face it head-on and use adversities for soul growth.

Ensouling Ourselves

Joan Borysenko

❧

The element of discovery is very important.

Portrait of Myself

The very secret of life for me . . . was to maintain in the midst of rushing events an inner tranquility.

Portrait of Myself

Margaret Bourke-White

❧

We are minor in everything but our passions.

Official Facebook page

Elizabeth Bowen

❧

When you take a stand out of deep conviction, people know. They may not even agree, but they ask, "Do I want someone who is willing to take a hard stand and someone I can trust to do that when the chips are down?" They want that.

Addressing the United States Senate

Barbara Boxer

The road that is built in hope is more pleasant to the traveler than the road built in despair, even though they both lead in the same direction.

The Fall of Atlantis

Marion Zimmer Bradley

ॐ

If we had no winter, the spring would not be so pleasant: if we did not sometimes taste of adversity, prosperity would not be so welcome.

Meditations Divine and Moral

Anne Bradstreet

ॐ

The most important factor in determining whether you will succeed isn't your gender, it's you. Take risks.

Bloomberg News

Angela Braly

ॐ

Those who live passionately teach us how to love. Those who love passionately teach us how to live.

Something More

Our deepest wishes are whispers of our authentic selves. We must learn to respect them. We must learn to listen.

Simple Abundance

Sarah Ban Breathnach

Optimism is joyful searching; pessimism is a prison of fear and a clutching at illusionary safety.

After the Darkest Hour

Kathleen A. Brehony

و

Let the world know you as you are, not as you think you should be, because sooner or later, if you are posing, you will forget the pose, and then where are you?

Funny Woman by Barbara W. Grossman

Fannie Brice

و

Things change whether you want them to, or not—unless you are dead. Don't hold so hard to the past that you die with it.

River Marked

Patricia Briggs

 و

I just try to accentuate the positive, and I don't try to point out the flaws.

People magazine

Some women follow every aging rule—like, after forty, you can't have a skirt above your knee. I prefer to focus on what I can do.

People magazine

Christie Brinkley

Look twice before you leap.

Life and Works of the Sisters Bronte

Remorse is the poison of life.

Jane Eyre

I would always rather be happy than dignified.

Jane Eyre

Life appears to me too short to be spent in nursing animosity and registering wrongs.

Jane Eyre

Charlotte Bronte

&

I've dreamt in my life dreams that have stayed with me ever after, and changed my ideas, they've gone through and through me, like wine through water, and altered the colour of my mind.

Wuthering Heights

Emily Bronte

&

With men passion is all at the beginning and with women it is all along.

The Paris Review

Real love is a pilgrimage. It happens when there is no strategy, but it is very rare because most people are strategists.

Women Writers Talk

You never know what you will learn till you start writing. Then you discover truths you never knew existed.

Journal for You

Anita Brookner

⚮

I didn't want to write about somebody who turned out to be a star 'cause most people don't turn out to be stars. And yet their lives are just as sweet and just as rich as any others and often they are richer and sweeter.

Maud Martha

Gwendolyn Brooks

⚮

The best proof of love is trust.

The Biography Channel

Anger repressed can poison a relationship as surely as the cruelest words.

Good Housekeeping magazine

A strong, positive self-image is the best possible preparation for success in life.

The Biography Channel

Success is a state of mind. If you want success, start thinking of yourself as a success.

The Biography Channel

Joyce Brothers

Belonging starts with self-acceptance . . . Believing that you're enough is what gives you the courage to be authentic.

O, The Oprah Magazine

Vulnerability is not about winning, and it's not about losing. It's about having the courage to show up and be seen.

O, The Oprah Magazine

Brene Brown

❧

Sexual attention from men is almost always flattering.

Finerman Rules

Beauty can't amuse you, but brainwork—reading, writing, thinking—can.

The Summer Everything Changed

Helen Gurley Brown

❧

Love is the wild card of existence.

In Her Day

He unzipped his pants and his brains fell out.

Venus Envy

When God made man she was practicing.

Cat on the Scent

Happiness is pretty simple: someone to love, something to do, something to look forward to.

Hiss of Death

Rita Mae Brown

ॐ

Earth's crammed with heaven

Aurora Leigh

Whoever loves true life, will love true love.

Aurora Leigh

Light tomorrow with today.

The Poetical Works of Elizabeth Barrett Browning

Elizabeth Barrett Browning

ॐ

I believe the old boys' network is a powerful one. No one gives up power and privilege willingly, do they?

The Daily Beast interview by Jesse Ellison

Quentin Bryce

ॐ

One faces the future with one's past.

What American Means to Me

Growth itself contains the gem of happiness.

To My Daughters, with Love

Pearl Buck

I'm a true believer in karma. You get what you give, whether it's bad or good.

The Charlie Rose Show

Falling in love-you should go with it, regardless of whether or not your heart gets smashed. You'll be a better person.

The Huffington Post

Sandra Bullock

ൟ

Feminism is an entire world view or gestalt, not just a laundry list of women's issues.

New Directions for Women

Charlotte Bunch

ൟ

Spirituality is a broad concept, transcending religious boundaries. By virtue of being human, all people are spiritual, regardless of whether or how they participate in religious observance.

Spirituality: Living Our Connectedness

Margaret A. Burkhardt

ൟ

I have always grown from my problems and challenges, from the things that don't work out, that's when I've really learned.

Ms. magazine

Carol Burnett

Where you are is not who you are.

YWCA, speech

You're not going to achieve perfect work/life balance every day or even every month. It's about having balance over longer periods of time. Don't be afraid to "check out" to put family first when necessary.

The Wall Street Journal

Ursula Burns

ᘍ

What a lovely surprise to discover how un-lonely being alone can be.

New Woman magazine

Ellen Burstyn

ᘍ

You know, to us, family means putting your arms around each other and being there.

Republican National Convention, 1992

Barbara Bush

ᘍ

Maybe our girlfriends are our soulmates and guys are just people to have fun with.

Sex and the City

Candace Bushnell

Teachers, I believe, are the most responsible and important members of society because their professional efforts affect the fate of the earth.

If You Love This Planet

Helen Caldicott

❧

Women are not pals enough with men, so we must make ourselves indispensable. After all, we have the greatest weapon in our hands by just being women.

Maria Callas by David Bret

Maria Callas

❧

What we focus on, we empower and enlarge. Good multiplies when focused upon. Negativity multiplies when focused upon. The choice is ours. Which do we want more of?

Blessings

Julia Cameron

❧

That which yields, is not always weak.

Kushiel's Dart

I have known the depths to which mortals are capable of descending, and I have seen the heights. I have seen how kindness and compassion may grow in the unlikeliest of places, as the mountain flower forces its way through the stern rock.

Kushiel's Dart

Jacqueline Carey

Little deeds of kindness, little words of love. Help to make earth happy, like the heaven above.

Little Things

Julia Carney

❧

In nature nothing exists alone.

Silent Spring

The more clearly we can focus our attention on the wonders and realities of the universe about us, the less taste we shall have for destruction.

Silent Spring

The human race is challenged more than ever before to demonstrate our mastery, not over nature but of ourselves.

SilentSpring.org

Rachel Carson

❧

I really hope I can make a difference. Even in the smallest way. I am looking forward to helping as much as I can.

The Biography Channel

Catherine, Duchess of Cambridge

❧

In the adjustment of the new order of things, we women demand an equal voice; we shall accept nothing less.

Women's Words by Mary Briggs

Service to a just cause rewards the worker with more real happiness and satisfaction than any other ventures of life.

Forbes magazine

Carrie Chapman Catt

ॐ

We need to empower women. Give women a voice in the decision-making process. Give women a political voice where they can champion, for their own welfare.

pbs.org

Margaret Chan

ॐ

A girl should be two things; classy and fabulous.

The Gospel According to Coco Chanel by Karen Karbo

The most courageous act is still to think for yourself. Aloud.

Believing in Ourselves by Armand Eisen

In order to be irreplaceable, one must always be different.

Woman's Day magazine

Gabrielle "Coco" Chanel

ॐ

Sensuality is complicated. Love is intricate. And the flesh is sweet, but I no longer mistake it for the whole thing.

The Decade of Women
by Suzanne Levine and Harriet Lyons

Chris Chase

Life itself is the proper binge.

Julia Child: A Life

Julia Child

❧

Women continue receiving less salary for the same kind of job. Women have a higher unemployment rate in our country. When you analyze the composition of poverty, you will find that most of the families in poverty are being run by a woman.

Forbes magazine

Laura Chinchilla

❧

I always thought that people told you that you're beautiful— that this was a title that was bestowed upon you . . . I think that it's time to take this power into our own hands and to say, "You know what? I'm beautiful. I just am. And that's my light. I'm just a beautiful woman.

Psychology Today magazine

Margaret Cho

❧

You can seduce a man without taking anything off, without even touching him.

The Huffington Post

Rea Dawn Chong

❧

Service is the rent that you pay for room on this earth.

I Dream a World by Brian Lanker

Shirley Chisholm

The bird that would soar above the level plain of tradition and prejudice must have strong wings.

The Awakening

Kate Chopin

&

I like living. I have sometimes been wildly, despairingly, acutely miserable, racked with sorrow, but through it all I still know quite certainly that just to be alive is a grand thing.

An Autobiography

Agatha Christie

&

You gotta believe in what you do—if you don't believe in it nobody else will.

Twitter, Official Ciara account

Education is everything—education is your power, education is your way in life for whatever you want to do.

Parade magazine

It won't always be the same, can't be afraid of change.

Twitter, Official Ciara account

Ciara (Ciara Princess Harris)

&

You can't forget the things you did in the past, or you'll never learn from them.

City of Fallen Angels

One must always be careful of books...and what is inside them, for words have the power to change us.

Clockwork Angel

Not everything that's true needs to be said.

City of Bones

Cassandra Clare

෯

I think sex education should include enhancing a girl's sexual self-image and self-esteem, and give her the tools to say "no," and ultimately "yes," when the time is right.

Book World live discussion

Anita H. Clayton

෯

Success is really a result of we.

YouTube: 60 Second Entrepreneur

Connie Clerici

෯

Fail to plan, plan to fail.

Living History

Laws and traditions that hold back women, hold back entire societies.

Speech from *Women in the World Summit*

We should remember that just as a positive outlook on life can promote good health, so can everyday acts of kindness.

It Takes a Village

We need to understand that there is no formula for how women should lead their lives. That is why we must respect the choices that each woman makes for herself and her family. Every woman deserves the chance to realize her God-given potential.

It Takes a Village

When women participate in politics, it ripples out to the entire society . . . Women are the world's most underused resource.

New York Magazine

Hillary Rodham Clinton

෨

I always say perspective, perseverance and passion.

Interview by Jeff Sheldon

I concentrate on living in the now.

SashaCohen.com

Alexandra Pauline "Sasha" Cohen

෨

Sex . . . or lack thereof . . . is at the center of everyone's identity, and once you've cracked someone's desires, you understand them in full.

Marie Claire magazine

A woman with a well-stocked toy drawer isn't dependent on anyone and is unlikely to hurl herself at a lowlife just for nooky.

Marie Claire magazine

Arianne Cohen

If folk can learn to be racist, they can learn to be antiracist. If being a sexist ain't genetic, then, dad gum, people can learn about gender equality.

I Dream a World by Brian Lanker

Your own words are the bricks and mortar of the dreams you want to realize. Your words are the greatest power you have. The words you choose and their use establish the life you experience.

Sonia Choquette

Johnnetta Betsch Cole

ও

Don't expect a job to be open-ended or last forever. Have a plan for where what you are doing right now is leading.

Finerman's Rules by Karen Finerman

Joanna Coles

ও

You will do foolish things, but do them with enthusiasm.

Concise Oxford Dictionary of Quotations
edited by Susan Ratcliff

What a wonderful life I've had! I only wish I'd realized it sooner.

Reflections of Helen by Gary Haun

Sidonie Gabrielle Colette

ও

The better you know yourself, the better your relationship with the rest of the world.

Woman's Day magazine

Toni Collette

How life catches up with us and teaches us to love and forgive each other.

Who Am I, Really?

Judy Collins

෨

Some walks you have to take alone.

Mockingjay

We can change. We can evolve as a species. It's not simple, and it's a very long and drawn-out process, but you can hope.

Interview by Rick Margolis

Suzanne Collins

෨

I don't run away from a challenge because I am afraid. Instead, I run toward it because the only way to escape fear is to trample it beneath your feet.

Letters to a Young Gymnast

Nadia Comaneci

෨

There is more difference within the sexes than between them.

Mother and Son

Ivy Compton-Burnett

෨

In order to deserve a true friend, we must learn first to be one.

Diamond Dust

A man's virtue should not be measured by his occasional exertions, but by his ordinary doings.

Diamond Dust

The happiness of life, like the light of day, consists not in one brilliant flash, but in a series of mild, serene rays.

Diamond Dust

Eliza Cook

ॐ

You have to speak your dream out loud.

O, The Oprah Magazine

Kelly Corrigan

ॐ

You can't please everyone, and you can't make everyone like you.

Ladies Home Journal

A boat is always safe in the harbor, but that's not what boats are built for.

The Best Advice I Ever Got

Katie Couric

ॐ

Life has taught me to be true to yourself. That being present in every moment is what's really important. To not be afraid to fail. To forgive.

Westlake Malibu Lifestyle magazine

Every single day is a juggling act: kids, work, exercise and, oh yeah, don't forget the husband. The key for me has been to be very organized, punctual, good at prioritizing, and developing an ability to say "no" sometimes. Modern life stretches us all a little thin.

Cindy.com

Cindy Crawford

ॐ

It's these turnaround or pivotal moments that introduce you to yourself . . . these small or these huge catastrophic events in your life—I do think that that's where you meet yourself.

Vanity Fair

I think love adds to everything. I'm an old softie about that. I think love is the most important thing in life. If you don't have [relationship], you're always looking for one. It's the motivator, the driver.

Dr. Drew Show interview

Sheryl Crow

ॐ

We are free up to the point of choice, and then the choice controls the chooser.

String of Pearls

Mary Crowley

ॐ

Nothing in life is to be feared, it is only to be understood. Now is the time to understand more, so that we may fear less.

Our Precarious Habitat by Melvin A. Benarde

Life is not easy for any of us. But what of that? We must have perseverance and above all confidence in ourselves. We must believe that we are gifted for something and that this thing must be attained.

Madame Curie by Eve Curie

You cannot hope to build a better world with out improving the individuals. To that end each of us must work for his own improvement, and at the same time share a general responsibility for all humanity, our particular duty being to aid those to who we think we can be most useful.

Pierre Curie translated by Charlotte Kellogg and Vernon Kellogg

Marie Curie

९०

Willpower is not some mythical force that we either have or don't have. Willpower is our decision to use higher-mind thinking instead of lazing around in the clutches of our primal mind.

Depression is a Choice

All my books carry the message: that kindness, civility, self-responsibility and a regard for the ceremonies of life lead us to a life of joy and healthy community with our fellows.

A. B. Curtiss, official website

A. B. Curtiss

९०

The greatest opportunities in life come with fear and risk.

Miles to Go

It is important to ask yourself why you're doing what you're doing and what purpose it serves in the big picture.

Miles to Go

Miley Cyrus

❧

If you've never been hated by your child, you've never been a parent.

Interview on CBS TV

Love is not enough. It must be the foundation, the cornerstone—but not the complete structure. It is much too pliable, too yielding.

The Lonely Life

Bette Davis

❧

No one is in control of your happiness but you; therefore, you have the power to change anything about yourself or your life that you want to change.

Real Moments

If we hold on to regret, we risk trapping ourselves in a prison of unrealized dreams from which it is difficult to escape.

How Did I Get Here?

Barbara De Angelis

❧

The world has improved mostly through people who are unorthodox, who do unorthodox things.

I Dream a World by Brian Lanker

The kind of beauty I want is the hard-to-get kind that comes from within—strength, courage, dignity.

Woman's Day magazine

Ruby Dee

~

My point is, life is about balance. The good and the bad. The highs and the lows. The pina and the colada.

Seriously . . . I'm Kidding

Beauty is about being comfortable in your own skin. It's about knowing and accepting who you are.

Seriously . . . I'm Kidding

If we don't want to define ourselves by things as superficial as our appearances, we're stuck with the revolting alternative of being judged by our actions.

My Point . . . And I Do Have One

I believe everything in life is energy. If we're destroying our trees and destroying our environment and hurting animals and hurting one another and all that stuff, there's got to be a very powerful energy to fight that. I think we need more love in the world. We need more kindness, more compassion, more joy, more laughter. I definitely want to contribute to that.

Good Housekeeping magazine

Ellen DeGeneres

Tattoos have a power and magic all their own. They decorate the body but they also enhance the soul.

Tattoo: The Exotic Art of Skin Decoration

Michelle Delio

&

Tattoos fulfill a need to inscribe the self as an individual.

Bodies of Inscription

Margo Demello

&

Relationships don't always make sense. Especially from the outside.

Along for the Ride

Sarah Dessen

&

It's not what other people believe you can do, it's what you believe.

Cable News Network

Gail Devers

&

If you find someone you love in life you must hang on to it and look after it.

The Biography Channel

Everyone needs to be valued. Everyone has the potential to give something back.

Time magazine

Carry out a random act of kindness, with no expectation of reward, safe in the knowledge that one day someone might do the same for you.

Random Acts of Kindness Then and Now

Diana, Princess of Wales

౨

I find ecstasy in living—the mere sense of living is joy enough.

Selected Poems of Emily Dickinson

We never know how high we are
Till we are called to rise
And then if we are true to plan
Our statures touch the skies.

From the poem "Life"

Emily Dickinson

౨

We tell ourselves stories in order to live.

The White Album

There's a point when you go with what you've got. Or you don't go.

Joan Didion: Essays and Conversations

Life changes fast. Life changes in the instant. You sit down to dinner and life as you know it ends.

The Year of Magical Thinking

Character—the willingness to accept responsibility for one's own life—is the source from which self-respect springs.

Slouching Towards Bethlehem

Joan Didion

♋

It's the friends you can call up at 4am that matter.

Glamour magazine

There is a gigantic difference between earning a great deal of money and being rich.

The Biography Channel

Marlene Dietrich

♋

The dedicated life is the life worth living. You must give with your whole heart.

Annie Dillard by Linda L. Smith

Annie Dillard

♋

Never go to bed mad. Stay up and fight.

Housekeeping Hints

A smile is a curve that sets everything straight.

Laffirmations

Always be nice to your children because they are the ones who will choose your rest home.

Like a Lampshade in a Whorehouse

Phyllis Diller

❧

So many persons think divorce a panacea for every ill, who find out, when they try it, that the remedy is worse.

Her Book

Dorothy Dix

❧

I prefer to explore the most intimate moments, the smaller, crystalized details we all hinge our lives on.

Ebony magazine

You have to imagine it possible before you can see something. You can have the evidence right in front of you, but if you can't imagine something that has never existed before, it's impossible.

Academy of Achievement video

Rita Dove

❧

I don't understand men. I don't even understand what I don't understand about men.

Are Men Necessary

Maureen Dowd

❧

Happiness—like love—is itself an attitude.

Choosing Happiness

Your attitude to life is far more important in determining your happiness than your money, appearance, social status or talent.

Choosing Happiness

Stephanie Dowrick

ॐ

When nothing is sure, everything is possible.

The Middle Ground

I don't see how you can go too far in the right direction.

Jerusalem the Golden

Too academic an education can inhibit the workings of the creative mind.

The Paris Review

Margaret Drabble

ॐ

My mom always says, "If you don't believe in something, you'll lose yourself completely."

Cosmopolitan magazine

Hilary Duff

ॐ

You were once wild here. Don't let them tame you!

The Politically Incorrect Guide to American History
by Thomas E. Woods

Isadora Duncan

Our earliest ancestors probably learned that loyalty was a valuable survival tool. In the jungle, the desert, or the open plains, loyalty to your tribe increased your chances of surviving harsh weather and an unreliable supply of food and water.

The Loyalty Advantage

Dianne M. Durkin

୨

Feminism is hated because women are hated. Anti-feminism is a direct expression of misogyny; it is the political defense of women hating.

Right-Wing Women

Andrea Dworkin

୨

Adventure is worthwhile in itself.

I Married Adventure

Courage is the price that life exacts for granting peace.

Amelia, My Courageous Sister by Muriel Earhart

A single act of kindness throws out roots in all directions, and the roots spring up and make new trees. The greatest work that kindness does to others is that it makes them kind themselves.

Magic City Morning Star

The more one does and sees and feels, the more one is able to do, and the more genuine may be one's appreciation of fundamental things like home, and love, and understanding companionship.

Soaring Wings by George Palmer Putnam

Amelia Earhart

Until women learn to want economic independence . . . and until they work out a way to get this independence without denying themselves the joys of love and motherhood, it seems to me feminism has no roots.

The Birth Control Review

Crystal Eastman

❧

One must never look for happiness: one meets it by the way.

The Wilder Shores of Love by Lesley Blanch

Isabelle Eberhardt

❧

Health is not a condition of matter, but of mind.

Science and Health

Mary Baker Eddy

❧

If we don't stand up for children, then we don't stand for much.

Congressional Record by Congress

Learn to be quiet enough to hear the genuine within yourself so that you can hear it in others.

The Measure of Success

If you don't like the way the world is, you change it. You have an obligation to change it. You just do it one step at a time.

What Would You Do If You Ran The World?

by Shelly Rachanow

Marian Wright Edelman

I just knew if it could be done, it had to be done, and I did it.

Still Missing by Susan Ware

Gertrude Ederle

૭

It sometimes requires courage to fly from danger.

Mademoiselle Panache

If we take care of the moments, the years will take care of themselves.

Mademoiselle Panache

The unaffected language of real feeling and benevolence is easily understood, and is never ridiculous.

Angelina

Maria Edgeworth

૭

Marriage is socialism among two people.

The Worst Years of Our Lives

Barbara Ehrenreich

૭

Everyone has different layers to who they are.

The Guardian, interview by Hannah Pool

Carmen Electra

Joy is the best wine.

Silas Marner

A woman's lot is made for her by the love she accepts.

Felix Holt, the Radical

I like not only to be loved, but to be told I am loved.

The Life of George Eliot by Nancy Henry

What do we live for, if it is not to make life less difficult for each other?

Scenes of Clerical Life

I'm not denyin' the women are foolish: God Almighty made 'em to match the men.

Adam Bebe

George Eliot (Mary Evans)

๛

There are long periods when life seems a small, dull round, a petty business with no point, and then suddenly we are caught up in some great event which gives us a glimpse of the solid and durable foundations of our existence.

National Broadcast by Queen Elizabeth

Elizabeth II

๛

A good time to laugh is anytime you can.

Move On

What I like most about change is that it's a synonym for "hope." If you are taking a risk, what you are really saying is "I believe in tomorrow and I will be part of it."

Fifty on Fifty by Bonnie Miller Rubin

Linda Ellerbee

ૐ

Be the heroine of your life, not the victim.

Wellesley College commencement speech

In my sex fantasy, nobody ever loves me for my mind.

Crazy Salad and Scribble Scribble

Nora Ephron

ૐ

I prefer to have some beliefs that don't make logical sense.

Love Medicine

What happens when you let an unsatisfactory present go on long enough? It becomes your entire history.

The Plague of Doves

We do know that no one gets wise enough to really understand the heart of another, though it is the task of our life to try.

The Bingo Palace

Louise Erdrich

ૐ

Words travel as swiftly as desire, so it is possible to send a message of love without them.

Swift as Desire

To know how to produce a work of art is to know how to discard the extraneous.

The Law of Love

Laura Esquivel

༒

We seal our fate with the choices we make.

Seal Our Fate

Gloria Estefan

༒

You are more powerful than you know; you are beautiful just as you are.

Interviewed by Marianne Schnall

Melissa Etheridge

༒

In the space of aloneness—and perhaps only there—a woman is free to admit and act on her own desires. It is where we have opportunity to discover that we are not a half but a sovereign whole.

On My Own

Florence Falk

༒

There is no waiting and no delayed gratification because yoga is both the means and the result, and the seed of all that is possible is present at the very beginning. This experience of stillness is possible in the first ten minutes of your first yoga class. It is possible in this very breath.

Yoga Mind, Body and Spirit

Donna Farhi

Desire is this absurdity that holds open the infinity of possibility. Ever optimistic, ever resourceful, desire tells us what it sees as it speeds ahead on its divine wings. What we cannot see, desire describes, and then it goads us to travel on until we have given birth to Joy.

The Wounding and Healing of Desire

Wendy Farley

ço

In the last fifteen years, I have seen vegetarianism go from the fringe to fashion to fact of life because it's healthy and worthy way to live.

The Big Book of Vegetarian

Kathy Farrell-Kingsley

ço

Ninety percent of leadership is the ability to communicate something people want.

State Government News by Council of State Governments

Women have begun to see that if I go through that doorway, I take everybody through it.

Dianne Feinstein by Jerry Roberts

Dianne Feinstein

ço

A closed mind is a dying mind.

Radio Broadcast, 1947

A woman can look both moral and exciting—if she also looks as if it was quite a struggle.

Reader's Digest magazine

Edna Ferber

∾

There were periods of my life when a lot of people didn't believe in me. I still had faith in myself. I really had to ask myself life questions. Where do I see myself in five years? Create a ladder for yourself, and walk up the steps. Climb the ladder.

Glamour magazine

I call my therapist every other day. It's not a one-stop shop. You have to push away all that negativity in your head. Face it, name it, let it go.

Marie Claire magazine

Fergie (Fergie Duhamel)

∾

Do your thing and don't care if they like it.

Bossypants

If you retain nothing else, always remember the most important Rule of Beauty. "Who cares?"

Bossypants

I think women especially, you need to have a plan. I need to have some other ways to generate income, so I don't have to stretch my face or lift the top of my head with surgery or something.

Bossypants

Tina Fey

I began to have an idea of my life, not as the slow shaping of achievement to fit my preconceived purposes, but as the gradual discovery and growth of a purpose which I did not know.

Pooling Blood by Cheryl Nineff D'Ambrosio

Jonna Field

༉

Let's face it—if mothers ruled the world, there wouldn't be any goddamn wars in the first place.

Emmy Awards acceptance speech

Sally Field

༉

If you don't proactively want success for yourself, how are you going to convince others that you're worthy of attaining it.

Finerman Rules

Karen Finerman

༉

Like love, chocolate is always a delight to receive or to give.

The Diabetic Chocolate Cookbook

Mary Jane Finsand

༉

I'm very sane about how crazy I am.

Wishful Drinking

Carrie Fisher

Sharing food with another human being is an intimate act that should not be indulged in lightly.

An Alphabet of Gourmets

M. F. K. Fisher

❧

Just don't give up trying to do what you really want to do.

Ella Fitzgerald by Katherine E. Krohn

Where there is love and inspiration, I don't think you can go wrong.

Ella Fitzgerald by Katherine E. Krohn

Ella Fitzgerald

❧

No two people see the external world in exactly the same way. To every separate person a thing is what he thinks it is—in other words, not a thing, but a think.

The Gate of Angels

Penelope Fitzgerald

❧

The first thing is to love your sport. Never do it to please someone else. It has to be yours.

The Champion's Mind by Jim Afremow

Peggy Fleming

❧

Compassion—that's the one thing no machine ever had. Maybe it's the one thing that keeps man ahead of them.

Star Trek: "The Ultimate Computer"

D. C. Fontana

Minor things can become moments of great revelation when encountered for the first time.

Margot Fonteyn: Autobiography

The one important thing I have learned over the years is the difference between taking one's work seriously and taking one's self seriously. The first is imperative and the second is disastrous.

Simpson's Contemporary Quotations
by James Beasely Simspon

Margot Fonteyn

ço

The search for human freedom can never be complete without freedom for women.

FordLibraryMuseum.go

I'll never forget the day that I was told to have a mastectomy. My reaction to the words was total denial.

CBS News

A housewife deserves to be honored as much as a woman who earns her living in the marketplace. I consider bringing up children a responsible job.

The Times of My Life

Betty Ford

ço

Finally I realized that dreams seldom materialize on their own.

Gorillas in the Mist

When you realize the value of all life, you dwell less on what is past and concentrate more on the preservation of the future.

Dian Fossey by Leah Jerome

The more you learn about the dignity of the gorilla, the more you want to avoid people.

Time magazine

Dian Fossey

ɷ

When you stop chasing the wrong things, you give the right things a chance to catch you.

Twitter, Official Megan Fox account

It's easy to just want to stay in because it's comfortable. But I think couples need to mix it up. When we go out to dinner, I find that I flirt with him in ways that I totally don't do in the comfort of our home.

Cosmopolitan magazine

Megan Fox

ɷ

Trouble is a sieve through which we sift our acquaintances. Those too big to pass through are our friends.

Hardware Dealers magazine

Arlene Francis

ɷ

Whoever is happy will make others happy too.

Diary of a Young Girl

In spite of everything I still believe that people are really good at heart.

Diary of a Young Girl

We all live with the objective of being happy; our lives are all different and yet the same.

Diary of a Young Girl

Everyone has inside of her a piece of good news. The good news is that you don't know how great you can be! How much you can love! What you can accomplish! And what your potential is.

Diary of a Young Girl

Anne Frank

❧

I'm always so excited about what I do that I try to get everyone to feel that way.

Los Angeles Times

Missy Franklin

❧

Science and everyday life cannot and should not be separated.

My Sister Rosalind Franklin by Jenifer Glynn

Rosaland Franklin

❧

When a man gets up to speak, people listen then look. When a woman gets up, people look, then, if they like what they see, they listen.

Mrs. Crankhurst by Jilly Cooper and Tom Hartman

Pauline Frederick

But from here, surveying the landscape of the latest scientific evidence for the build effect, I say with confidence: positivity can change your life.

Positivity

Any positive emotion can draw you to smile and carry yourself with a more open posture. And so any positive emotion can be taken by those around you as a sign to relax and connect.

Love 2.0

Barbara L. Fredrickson

ॐ

To nourish children and raise them against odds is in any time, any place, more valuable than to fix bolts in cars or design nuclear weapons.

Woman to Woman by Julia Gilden and Mark Friedman

Marilyn French

ॐ

It takes a disciplined person to listen to convictions which are different from their own.

A Thousand Friends

Dorothy Fuldheim

ॐ

If you have knowledge, let others light their candles in it.

Woman's Day magazine

Margaret Fuller

Love is a game that two can play and both win.

Reader's Digest magazine

Eva Gabor

ॐ

Husbands are like fires. They go out when unattended.

Newsweek magazine

Zsa Zsa Gabor

ॐ

It's cooler to be strong.

M.A.C.'s VIVA Glam Event

I think it's ok to be confident in yourself.

Vogue magazine

You have to be unique, and different, and shine in your own way.

My Brother's Keeper

If you don't have any shadows you're not in the light.

MTV News

Lady Gaga

ॐ

You must learn to be still in the midst of activity and to be vibrantly alive in repose.

People magazine

Indira Gandhi

Together we can face any challenges as deep as the ocean and as high as the sky.

Official Facebook page

Sonia Gandhi

ℰ

You don't have to be married to have a good friend as your partner for life.

Conversations with Greta Garbo
by Sven Broman and Greta Garbo

Greta Garbo

ℰ

Everyone should say what they wanted. It saves time.

The Perfect Husband

Lisa Gardner

ℰ

A woman with a voice is by definition a strong woman. But the search to find that voice can be remarkably difficult.

Woman's Day magazine

Melinda Gates

ℰ

I want to be judged on my own merits.

Time magazine

Different times need different types of leadership.

Los Angles Times

Park Geun-hye

I am not a hero but did what seemed necessary at the time.

MiepGies.com

People should never think that you have to be a very special person to help those who need you.

The Biography Channel

Permanent remorse about failing to do your human duty, in my opinion, can be worse than losing your life.

Scholastic interview

Miep Gies

ॐ

Stop wearing your wishbone where your backbone ought to be.

Eat, Pray, Love

People think a soul mate is your perfect fit, and that's what everyone wants. But a true soul mate is a mirror, the person who shows you everything that is holding you back, the person who brings you to your own attention so you can change your life.

Eat, Pray, Love

To be fully seen by somebody, then, and be loved anyhow—this is a human offering that can border on miraculous.

Committed

Elizabeth Gilbert

ॐ

Hold up your head! You were not made for failure, you were made for victory.

Anne Gilchrist: Her Life and Writings

Anne Gilchrist

We live at the level of our language. Whatever we can articulate we can imagine or understand or explore.

Falling Through Space

Ellen Gilchrist

❧

America has always understood this principle of the economy— that everyone can benefit when everyone competes.

Address to a Joint Session of Congress

Julia Gillard

❧

My mother told me to be a lady. And for her, that meant be your own person, be independent.

Wagner University, faculty.wagner.edu

Women will only have true equality when men share with them the responsibility of bringing up the next generation.

Wagner University, faculty.wagner.edu

I said on the equality side of it, that it is essential to a woman's equality with man that she be the decision-maker, that her choice be controlling.

The New York Times

Ruth Bader Ginsburg

❧

We love because it's the only true adventure.

Ebony magazine

Art is not for the cultivated taste. It is to cultivate taste.

A Poetic Equation

Mistakes are a fact of life. It is the response to the error that counts.

Black Feeling, Black Talk, Black Judgement

Nikki Giovanni

༄

What you get is a living—what you give is a life.

Lillian Gish by Stuart Oderman

Lillian Gish

༄

No life is so hard that you can't make it easier by the way you take it.

Life and Gabriella
by Ellen Anderson and Gholson Glasgow

Ellen Glasgow

༄

Philosophy should quicken life, not deaden it.

Little Masks

What men have thought about life in the past is less important than what you feel about it to-day.

Little Masks

Susan Glaspell

The race of children possess magically sagacious powers!

Dream Children

One is taught by experience to put a premium on those few people who can appreciate you for what you are.

The Finishing School

Gail Godwin

୭

Apathy—not hate—is the opposite of love. It is this apathy that leads first to the death of the psyche, and in its extreme form to the death of the body.

The Dark Side of Love

Jane G. Goldberg

୭

If love does not know how to give and take without restrictions, it is not love, but a transaction that never fails to lay stress on a plus and a minus.

The Tragedy of Woman's Emancipation

The history of progress is written in the blood of men and women who have dared to espouse an unpopular cause, as, for instance, the black man's right to his body, or woman's right to her soul.

What I Believe

Idealists . . . foolish enough to throw caution to the wind . . . have advanced mankind and have enriched the world.

Living My Life

Emma Goldman

We have the choice to use the gift of our life to make the world a better place.

JaneGoodall.org

Only if we understand, can we care. Only if we care, we will help. Only if we help, we shall be saved.

Jane Goodall: 40 Years at Gombe

We have so far to go to realize our human potential for compassion, altruism, and love.

Harvest for Hope

You cannot get through a single day without having an impact on the world around you. What you do makes a difference, and you have to decide what kind of difference you want to make.

Planet Savers by Kevin Desmond

Jane Goodall

ॐ

Avoid retirement playgrounds like poison, because that's exactly what they are.

Linda Goodman's Star Signs

Linda Goodman

ॐ

The truth isn't always beauty, but the hunger for it is.

A Bolter and the Invincible Summer

Nadine Gordimer

Courage is like a muscle. We strengthen it by use.

L'Officiel magazine

Ruth Gordo

Each person has his own safe place—running, painting, swimming, fishing, weaving, gardening. The activity itself is less important than the act of drawing on your own resources.

Winning Life's Toughest Battles by Julius Segal

Barbara Gordon

Respect . . . is appreciation of the separateness of the other person, of the ways in which he or she is unique.

Reader's Digest magazine

Annie Gottlieb

Once, power was considered a masculine attribute. In fact, power has no sex.

Cosmopolitan magazine

Katherine Graham

Dance is the hidden language of the soul.

The New York Times

There is only one of you in all time, this expression is unique. And if you block it, it will never exist through any other medium and it will be lost.

*Said to Agnes Miller after
the 1943 opening of Oklahoma*

Martha Graham

క

I'm in motion and that's fine with me. The only thing I don't want is boredom. I don't mind being up or down, I just don't want to be still.

The Hollywood Reporter

Lee Grant

క

Friendship is by its very nature freer of deceit than any other relationship we can know because it is the bond least affected by striving for power, physical pleasure, or material profit, most liberated from any oath of duty or of constancy. With Eros the body stands naked, in friendship our spirit is denuded.

Adam and Eve and the City

Francine du Plessix Gray

క

The essence of pleasure is spontaneity.

The Female Eunuch

Germaine Greer

To have a reason to get up in the morning, it is necessary to possess a guiding principle. A belief of some kind.

Ordinary People

Judith Guest

&

Hands that never touch. Lips that never meet. The Almost Lovers, never to be.

Frankie's Monster

Rae Hachton

&

Morning . . . 'tis Nature's gayest hour!

Summer Morning

Sarah Josepha Hale

&

In accepting death as inevitable, we don't label it as a good thing or a bad thing. As one of my teachers once said to me, "Death happens. It is just death, and how we meet it is up to us."

Being with Dying

Joan Halifax

&

The clearer and happier you feel inside, the more joyous and loving your outer world becomes because love attracts love.

Love Crystals

Judy Hall

Hindsight is of little value in the decision-making process. It distorts our memory for events that occurred at the time of the decision so that the actual consequence seems to have been a "foregone conclusion." Thus, it may be difficult to learn from our mistakes.

Thought and Knowledge

Diane F. Halpern

ೞ

The people who say you are not facing reality actually mean that you are not facing their idea of reality. Reality is above all else a variable. With a firm enough commitment, you can sometimes create a reality which did not exist before.

No Laughing Matter

Margaret Halsey

ೞ

When in doubt, take a deep breath and keep moving.

Guilty Pleasures

The only true happiness lies in knowing who you are . . . and making peace with it.

Narcissus in Chains

Sex was never as neat as the movies made it. Real sex was messy. Good sex was messier.

Blue Moon

If you love someone, then your freedom is curtailed. If you love someone, you give up much of your privacy. If you love someone, then you are no longer merely one person but half of a couple. To think or behave any other way is to risk losing that love.

Obsidian Butterfly

Laurell K. Hamilton

ᆨ

Confidence is a natural life force designed to overcome dark times.

Complete Confidence

Sheenah Hankin

ᆨ

There is always something left to love. And if you ain't learned that, you ain't learned nothing.

A Raisin in the Sun

Lorraine Hansberry

ᆨ

When I feel like I'm not doing what I am supposed to as a mother, I will torture myself. I don't know how to deal with it. I find some consolation in the fact that all mommies feel it. If there was a way to cure mommy guilt. I would bottle it and be a bazzillionaire.

Good Housekeeping magazine

Angie Harmon

The respect that is only bought by gold is not worth much.

A Brighter Coming Day:
A Frances Ellen Watkins Harper Reader

Frances Harper

୬

Happiness. Simple as a glass of chocolate or tortuous as the heart. Bitter Sweet. Alive.

Chocolat

Life is what you celebrate. All of it. Even its end.

Chocolat

Joanne Harris

୬

Those who start out as outcasts can wind up as being part of the system.

Newsweek magazine

Patricia Roberts Harris

୬

Those who do not have imaginary conversations do not love.

The Stillest Day

Sometimes we need a map of the past. It helps us to understand the present, and plan the future.

Damage

We learn from tragedy. Slowly.

The Truth About Love

Josephine Hart

Self-esteem is as important to our well-being as legs are to a table. It is essential for physical and mental health and for happiness.

The Winning Family

Louise Hart

ॐ

There's no magic bullet; there's no pill that makes everything great and makes you happy all the time. I'm letting go of those expectations, and that's opening me up to moments of transcendent bliss.

Glamour magazine

Anne Hathaway

ॐ

I have witnessed the softening of the hardest of hearts by a simple smile.

The Biography Channel

The only thing that will make you happy is being happy with who you are, and not who people think you are.

GoldieHawn.co.uk

I've come to believe that seeking happiness is not a frivolous pursuit. It's honorable and necessary. And most people forget even to think about it.

O, The Oprah Magazine

Goldie Hawn

ॐ

Love is the great miracle cure. Loving ourselves works miracles in our lives.

You Can Heal Your Life

The point of power is always in the present moment.

Heal Your Body

I say "Out" to every negative thought that comes to my mind.

Life!

Your unique creative talents and abilities are flowing through you and are being expressed in deeply satisfying ways. Your creativity is always in demand.

Everyday Positive Thinking

Louise L. Hay

༄

The story of a love is not important—what is important is that one is capable of love. It is perhaps the only glimpse we are permitted of eternity.

Guideposts

People who refuse to rest honorably on their laurels when they reach "retirement" age seem very admirable to me.

My Life in Three Acts

Helen Hayes

༄

The married are those who have taken the terrible risk of intimacy and, having taken it, know life without intimacy to be impossible.

Ms. magazine

Carolyn Heilbrun

You don't always know how to do things when they're happening.

Another Part of the Forest

Nothing, of course, begins at the time you think it did.

An Unfinished Woman

Lillian Hellman

જી

There is definitely a double standard for men and women: When a man loses his temper, he is aggressive; I'm a pushy bitch. A man is confident and authoritative; I'm conceited and power-mad. Men don't want women getting to the top.

Playboy magazine

Leona Helmsley

જી

You can turn just about any simple act into a practice of mindfulness, and it will nurture and nourish you; it will start your day off in a positive way.

Running with Nature

Mariel Hemingway

જી

One thing I have learned is that I can get interesting results if I start at the point of most contentment, the most satisfying moment, instead of the most jeopardy.

The Paris Review

They say the smart dog obeys but the smarter dog knows when to disobey.

In the Cemetery Where Al Jolson is Buried
Amy Hempel

ᕫ

Sometimes we know who we want to be and what we want to do long…long before we know how to get there.

Between the Tides
Patti Callahan Henry

ᕫ

The best thing to hold onto in life is each other.

Audrey Hepburn by Yann-Brice Dherbier

The most important thing is to enjoy your life—to be happy—it's all that matters.

Vogue magazine

Elegance is the only beauty that never fades.

Marie Claire magazine

Nothing is impossible. The word itself says, 'I'm possible!'

The Biography Channel

People, even more than things, have to be restored, renewed, revived, reclaimed, and redeemed; never throw out anyone.

Building in Research and Evaluation
by Yoland Wadsworth
Audrey Hepburn

Without discipline, there's no life at all.

> *The Hidden Gifts of the Introverted Child* by Marti Olsen Laney

If you obey all the rules, you miss all the fun.

> *Katharine Hepburn Once Said* by Susan Crimp

As one goes through life one learns that if you don't paddle your own canoe, you don't move.

> *Me: Stories of My Life*

Katharine Hepburn

∽

I'm really proud to be a part, in whatever way, of women becoming more active in the political scene.

> Interview by Katie Couric

Anita Hill

∽

In the Primordial Age Woman Was Once the Sun!

> *Seito*

Raicho Hiratsuka

∽

Words are not the end of thought, they are where it begins.

> *After Long Silence*

Solitude, whether endured or embraced, is a necessary gateway to original thought.

> *Nine Gates*

Poems want to awaken intimacy, connection, expansion, and wildness.

Words with Writers, interview

Jane Hirshfield

ৎ

I'm suggesting we call sex something else, and it should include everything from kissing to sitting close together.

Public Broadcasting Station

Shere Hite

ৎ

Condemn not truth for error's deeds.

Flowers and Weeds

For though time may seem to drag slowly on.
Before you will know it, time will be gone.

The Voice of the Clock

Life is the root of Eden's loftiest tree.
Whose ripened fruit is immortality.

God's Gift to Man

Martha Lavinia Hoffman

ৎ

Childbirth, after all, turns life upside down. Whereas previously the couple had to nurture only each other, now they are part of a triad. Their entire balance of forces must be recast. Furthermore, this must be negotiated at a time of sleep deprivation, physical exhaustion, and economic pressure. Now wonder couples have difficulty.

Women's Stories of Divorce at Childbirth

Hilary Hoge

While there is life there is hope—and while there is hope there is life.

Joyful Through Hope

E. E. Holmes

ം

How can hope be false when it is as much a part of the human experience as birth or death?

Help Me Live

We can have hope even while maintaining a negative—or sometimes simply realistic—attitude. For instance, if you're dying of cancer, you can still hope for pain relief. If you have a difficult-to-treat cancer, you can still hope for new treatments.

Help Me Live

Lori Hope

ം

When you have a good idea and you've tried it and you know it's going to work, go ahead and do it—because it's much easier to apologize afterwards than it is to get permission.

Grace Hopper by Kathleen Broome Williams

Grace Hopper

ം

Don't be afraid to feel as angry or as loving as you can, because when you feel nothing, it's just death.

I Dream a World by Brian Lanker

Lena Horne

"I think patience is what love is," he said, "because how could you love somebody without it?"

A Different Woman

New links must be forged as old ones rust.

A Different Woman

Jane Howard

ॐ

Don't you think that the best things are already in view?

What is Religion?

Julia Ward Howe

ॐ

This is the essence of beauty—the possession of a quality which excites the human organism to functioning harmonious with its own nature.

The Psychology of Beauty

Ethel Puffer Howes

ॐ

The function of knowledge is to transcend earthly experience, not wallow in it.

The Society of S

Man's sole duty is to produce as much pleasure as possible.

The Society of S

Susan Hubbard

Confidence is key. Sometimes, you need to look like you're confident even when you're not.

Seventeen magazine

Vanessa Hudgens

ॐ

No child is immune to peer pressure.

Raising Kids God's Way

You can't lose something you never had.

As Andie Anderson in the movie,
How to Lose a Guy in 10 Days

Kate Hudson

ॐ

I studied, I met with medical doctors, scientists, and I'm here to tell you that the way to a more productive, more inspired, more joyful life is: getting enough sleep . . . We are literally going to sleep our way to the top.

Ted Talks, Ted.com

Women still have an uneasy relationship with power and the traits necessary to be a leader. There is this internalized fear that if we are really powerful, we are going to be considered ruthless or pushy or strident—all those epithets that strike right at our femininity. We are still working at trying to overcome the fear that power and womanliness are mutually exclusive.

Newsweek magazine

Arianna Huffington

Beauty is in the eye of the beholder.

Molly Brown

Margaret Wolfe Hungerford

ൟ

If people are informed they will do the right thing. It's when they are not informed that they become hostages to prejudice.

I Dream a World by Brian Lanker

Charlayne Hunter-Gault

ൟ

Sex is discovery.

Anatomy of Me

Fannie Hurst

ൟ

Travel is the soul of civilization.

The Art of Pilgrimage

Loves makes your soul crawl out from its hiding place.

Their Eyes Were Watching God

Mama exhorted her children at every opportunity to "jump at de sun." We might not land on the sun, but at least we would get off the ground.

Dust Tracks on a Road

Zora Neale Hurston

You do not have a soul. You are a soul.

O, The Oprah Magazine

India.Arie (India Arie Simpson)

౿

Fashion is one of the great living arts of civilization and self-decoration one of the fundamental human urges.

A Fashion Alphabet

Janey Ironside

౿

I used to believe that anything was better than nothing. Now I know that sometimes nothing is better.

Ms. magazine

Glenda Jackson

౿

It is easy to be independent when you've got money. But to be independent when you haven't a thing—that's the Lord's test.

Downbeat—The Great Jazz Interviews

Mahalia Jackson

౿

Men aren't really complicated . . . They are very simple, literal creatures. They usually mean what they say. And we spend hours trying to analyze what they've said, when really it's obvious.

Fifty Shades of Grey

E. L. James

The best sex takes place in the mind.

How to Make Love Like a Porn Star

My definition of courage is never letting anyone define you.

Esquire magazine

Jenna Jameson

৵

It seems to me highly improbable that women are going to realize their human potential without alienating men—some men, anyway.

Cross Sections from a Decade of Change

Elizabeth Janeway

৵

The only way to get rid of the fear of doing something is to go out . . . and do it.

Feel the Fear and Do It Anyway

Susan J. Jeffers

৵

Very few women wait for Mr. Right. Most women take the first and worst Mr. Wrong.

The Piano Teacher

Only he who loves and is loved for his own sake can be happy, and what produces that happiness is not so much the sense of sexual communion as of two people being together . . . the sexual act viewed as a whole probably affords less happiness than a totally ordinary kiss or often one simple word from the one you love.

Wonderful, Wonderful Times

Elfriede Jelinek

Never limit yourself because of other's limited imagination; never limit others because of your own limited imagination.

The Biography Channel

The biggest challenge we all face is to learn about ourselves and to understand our strengths and weaknesses.

teacher.scholastic.com interview

I realized I would feel comfortable anywhere in the universe because I belonged to and was a part of it, as much as any star, planet, asteroid, comet or nebula.

teacher.scholastic.com interview

Mae C. Jemison

❧

Yoga heals, nourishes, and challenges us. The practice infiltrates every corner of our lives.

How We Live Our Yoga

Valerie Jeremijenko

❧

I'm happiest when I have something to focus my energy on.

ScarlettJohansson.org

It's so difficult to feel comfortable in the body you have. You always want to look a different way, taller or thinner, whatever it may be. I still struggle with it. I think everybody does.

Seventeen magazine

I do think on some basic level we are animals and by instinct we kind of breed accordingly. But, as much as I believe that, I work really hard when I'm in a relationship to make it work in a monogamous way.

London Telegraph

Scarlett Johansson

ॐ

Never let a problem to be solved become more important than a person to be loved.

The Joy Journal

Barbara Johnson

ॐ

Failing in life is inevitable—staying down is optional.

Women's Health magazine

Carrie Johnson

ॐ

Tea beckons us to enjoy quality time with friends and loved ones, and especially to rediscover the art of relaxed conversation.

Tea and Etiquette

Dorothea Johnson

ॐ

Always concentrate on how far you have come, rather than how far you have left to go. The difference in how easy it seems will amaze you.

Woman's Day magazine

Heidi Johnson

I want to encourage every woman, especially if you have a family history of breast or ovarian cancer, to seek out information and medical experts who can help you through this aspect of your life, and to make your own informed choices.

The New York Times

I'd like all girls to go to school. That's what we need to be thinking about, and working on making our own families good and strong and our own kids happy.

Today Show interview

Angelina Jolie

ॐ

If you're not having fun, then what the hell are you doing? It reminds me to find the reason why I'm doing it and why I'm out there, which makes things more manageable when I'm stressed and fatigued.

Women's Health magazine

Allison Jones

ॐ

You take your life in your own hands, and what happens? A terrible thing, no one to blame.

How to Save Your Own Life

Everyone has talent. What's rare is the courage to follow it to the dark places where it leads.

New York Quarterly

Show me a woman who doesn't feel guilty and I'll show you a man.

Fear of Flying

I have accepted fear as a part of life—specifically the fear of change . . . I have gone ahead despite the pounding in the heart that says turn back.

Sacred Selfishness by Bud Harris

Erica Jong

ॐ

My new found meaning of Marriage is a place where you can be yourself and has breathing space to grow personally and spiritually as and when I want without having to consult my partner about my changes.

Unconventional and Spiritual Marriage

Jeanette de Jonk

ॐ

Don't compromise yourself. You are all you've got.

He's Gone . . . You're Back

Janis Joplin

ॐ

I am telling young people that if you're dissatisfied . . . with the way things are, then you have got to resolve to change them.

I Dream a World by Brian Lanker

Barbara Jordan

I like being unconventional.

Ms. magazine

Florence Griffith Joyner

ﻬ

It is better to look ahead and prepare than to look back and regret.

Letters to a Young Sister by Hill Harper

Jackie Joyner-Kersee

ﻬ

Experience gives us the tests first and the lessons later.

Public Radio interview

No one's born with their destiny stamped on their forehead . . . we make the choices to fulfill our destiny.

Naomi's Breakthrough Guide

Naomi Judd

ﻬ

Flexibility is one of the key ingredients to being successful. If you feel like it's difficult to change, you will probably have a harder time succeeding.

You Can Do It! by Shelley Dudley

Andrea Jung

ﻬ

Love makes a family.

Love Makes a Family.

Gigi Kaeser

Nothing is worth more than laughter. It is strength to laugh and to abandon oneself, to be light. Tragedy is the most ridiculous thing.

FridaKahlo.org

Frida Kahlo

ה

Change demands new learning.

The Change Masters

Our future will be shaped by the assumptions we make about who we are and what we can be.

America the Principled

Confidence is the bridge connecting expectations and performance, investment and results.

Confidence

Rosabeth Moss Kanter

ה

Delete the negative; accentuate the positive!

Marie Claire magazine

Everything I do is a matter of heart, body and soul.

DonnaKaran.com

That I'm a woman makes me want to nurture others, fulfill needs and solve problems.

DonnaKaran.com

Donna Karan

Prostitution exists today because women are objectified sexually, and because it is considered more permissible for men than for women to have purely sexual experiences.

Common Women

Ruth Mazo Karras

᪣

I think it's important to keep mantras fresh (sometimes the same verse can get stale). That being said, I love this powerful statement: 'Define yourself.' I rehearsed it a million times during the 2005 Chicago Marathon [her first win].

Women's Health magazine

Deena Kastor

᪣

Literature is my utopia.

The Story of My Life

Optimism is the faith that leads to achievement; nothing can be done without hope.

Optimism

One can never consent to creep when one feels an impulse to soar.

The Story of My Life

Face your deficiencies and acknowledge them; but do not let them master you. Let them teach you patience, sweetness, insight.

Out of the Dark

The Bible gives me a deep, comforting sense that "things seen are temporal and things unseen are eternal."

The Story of My Life

Security is mostly superstition. It does not exist in nature, nor do the children of men as a whole experience it. Avoiding danger is no safer in the long run than outright exposure. Life is either a daring adventure or nothing.

The Open Door

Thus it is that my friends have made the story of my life. In a thousand ways they have turned my limitations into beautiful privileges, and enabled me to walk serene and happy in the shadow cast by my deprivation.

The Story of My Life

Helen Keller

ॐ

They frequently find the truth who do not seek it, they who do, frequently lose it.

Further Records, 1848-1883

Fanny Kemble

ॐ

It is hard to fight an enemy who has outposts in your head.

Esquire magazine

Sally Kempton

Solitude is the soul's holiday, an opportunity to stop doing for others and to surprise and delight ourselves instead.

KatrinaKenison.com

Katrina Kenison

ی

As much as we need a prosperous economy, we also need a prosperity of kindness and decency.

ABC News

I think my mother . . . made it clear that you have to live life by your own terms and you have to not worry about what other people think and you have to have the courage to do the unexpected.

The Telegraph newspaper

Caroline Kennedy

ی

If men could get pregnant, abortion would be a sacrament.

Ms. magazine

Florynce R. Kennedy

ی

Rigid beliefs make disappointments seem unbearable, whereas realistic beliefs help us to accept disappointment and go on from there.

The Unwritten Rules of Friendship

Eileen Kennedy-Moore

Flowers grow out of dark moments.

1 Message by Mary Lennox

Corita Kent

ᦒ

To know who you are is the greatest power of all.

Blood Trinity

Sherrilyn Kenyon and Dianna Love

ᦒ

Personally, I think if a woman hasn't met the right man by the time she's twenty-four, she may be lucky.

Essentials for Health and Wellness,
edited by Gordon Edlin

Deborah Kerr

ᦒ

You have to have a sense of humor about life to get through it.

Glamour Magazine

Every weird thing about you is beautiful and makes life interesting.

Rolling Stone iMagazine

Kersha (Bailey)

ᦒ

Love is moral even without legal marriage, but marriage is immoral without love.

The Morality of Woman

Ellen Key

Every little thing wants to be loved.

The Secret Life of Bees

The hardest thing on earth is choosing what matters

The Secret Life of Bees

Sue Monk Kidd

∽

I kept looking for happiness, and then I realized. This is it. It's a moment, and it comes, and it goes, and it'll come back again. I yearn for things, but at the same time I'm just peaceful.

Vanity Fair magazine

Nicole Kidman

∽

A man should kiss his wife's navel every day.

Nell Kimball
by Nell Kimball and Stephen Longstreet

Nell Kimball

∽

Remember, we all stumble, every one of us. That's why it's a comfort to go hand in hand.

The Innocents from Indiana

Emily Kimbrough

∽

Champions adjust to the situation. And they keep playing until they get it right.

Shape Your Self by Martina Navratilova

I think self-awareness is probably the most important thing towards being a champion.

The Sportswoman magazine

The main thing is to care. Care very hard, even if it is only a game you are playing.

Billie Jean

If your partner wants to be private, you have to respect that.

Esquire magazine

Billie Jean King

༜

I know for sure that nothing is guaranteed. Life always changes.

ABC News

When people don't want the best for you, they are not the best for you.

O, The Oprah Magazine

She has all the qualities you would want in a spouse. Somebody who is successful, who cheers you on, understands you, cares about you, supports you, who's honest with you.

The New York Times

Gayle King

༜

In the end nothing we do or say in this lifetime will matter as much as the way we have loved one another.

True Love

Weddings remind us that our lives have meaning and that love is the strongest bond, the happiest joy, and the loveliest healing we can ever experience.

Weddings from the Heart

Daphne Rose Kingma

෨

Small change, small wonders—these are the currency of my endurance and ultimately of my life. It's a workable economy.

Small Wonder

What I want is so simple, I almost can't say it: elementary kindness.

Animal Dreams

The very least you can do in your life is figure out what you hope for. And the most you can do is live inside that hope. Not admire it from a distance but live right in it, under its roof.

Animal Dreams

Barbara Kingsolver

෨

To me success means effectiveness in the world, that I am able to carry my ideas and values into the world—that I am able to change it in positive ways.

Official Facebook page

Maxine Hong Kingston

We can only accept friendship from others to the degree that we give it to ourselves.

On Friendship: A Book for Teenagers

Kimberly Kirberger

ఛ

I bring a lot of passion to my life and my politics—I don't mind saying there is a very strong Latin component to it.

Time magazine

Cristina Fernandez de Kirchner

ఛ

Clothes aren't going to change the world, the women who wear them will.

Marie Claire magazine

Anne Klein

ఛ

Feelings of love and gratitude arise directly and spontaneously in the baby in response to the love and care of his mother.

Love, Hate and Reparation

Melanie Klein

ఛ

A man's vanity is more fragile than you might think. It's easy for us to mistake shyness for coldness, and silence for indifference.

Devil in Winter

Lisa Kleypas

Women tend to be problem solvers. We work together.

CBS News

Amy Klobuchar

❦

What is important to a relationship is a harmony of emotional roles and not too great a disparity in the general level of intelligence.

Women in a Modern World

Mirra Komarovsky

❦

Feminism is the radical notion that women are human beings.

A Feminist Dictionary

Cheris Kramerae

❦

Grief is real because loss is real. Each grief has its own imprint, as distinctive and as unique as the person we lost.

On Grief and Grieving

The ultimate lesson all of us have to learn is unconditional love, which includes not only others but ourselves as well.

The Wheel of Life

It is only when we truly know and understand that we have a limited time on Earth and that we have no way of knowing when our time is up that we will begin to live each day to the fullest, as if it were the only one we had.

ekrfoundation.org

Elizabeth Kubler-Ross

There must be a goal at every stage of life! There must be a goal!

GrayPanthers.org

Stand before the people you fear and speak your mind—even if your voice shakes.

No Stone Unturned

Maggie Kuhn

↶

Peace is not the law imposed by the mighty, but that which is founded on equality and dignity of all peoples.

Speech to UNESCO delegates

Chandrika Kumaratunga

↶

If you have nothing in life but a good friend, you're rich.

The Winning Attitude

Don't close any doors unless you want them closed.

ESPN

Michelle Kwan

↶

I love cooking. Not for myself alone. Cooking is about giving.

The Independent, U. K. newspaper

When my father passed away and then when later on I gave birth, those are sort of ground-breaking experiences that put everything else into perspective.

CBS, *60 Minutes*

My father passed away when I was 16 . . . I was witness to a woman who single handedly brought up the entire family and managed to do everything…She was an extraordinary role model for me.

Forbes magazine

Christine Lagarde

೪

Take a chance and dream. Pursue something you love and be willing to spend the time and energy on it. You'll be amazed at what might happen.

my.steamboat.com

Whatever your dream is, know that there are going to be hard days in your life. You have to be prepared to fight.

Steamboat Today

Caroline Lalive

೪

You get your confidence and intuition back by trusting yourself, by being militantly on you own side.

Bird by Bird

The best way to change the world is to change your mind, which often requires feeding yourself . . . It's almost like a prayer: to be needy, to eat, taste, to be filled, building up instead of tearing down.

Grace

Anne Lamott

Expect trouble as an inevitable part of life and repeat to yourself, the most comforting words of all: This, too, shall pass.

The Ann Landers Encyclopedia, A to Z

Ann Landers (Eppie Lederer)

&

A penny saved is not a penny earned if at the end of the day you still owe a quarter.

Landrieu.senate.gov

Mary L. Landrieu

&

I believe that what we call beautiful is generally a by-product.

Dorothea Lange by Linda Gordon

Dorothea Lange

&

Life is short, wear your party pants!

Life is Short, Wear Your Party Pants

Loretta LaRoche

&

Look for a sweet person. Forget rich.

The New Yorker magazine

The most beautiful face in the world? It's yours.

EsteeLauder.com

I never dreamed about success. I worked for it.

The Biography Channel

Estee Lauder

I have always looked for ways to give back because I think it's a responsibility we all share.

The Avril Lavigne Foundation

Avril Lavigne

ৎ

Basically, I have been compelled by curiosity.

London Times

I had never passed a single school exam, and clearly never would.

Women in World History,
by Anne Commire

Mary Leakey

ৎ

Think before you speak. Read before you think.

The Fran Lebowitz Reader

Food is an important part of a balanced diet.

The Fran Lebowitz Reader

Fran Lebowitz

ৎ

The one thing that doesn't abide by majority rule is a person's conscience.

To Kill a Mockingbird

Until I feared I would lose it, I never loved to read. One does not love breathing.

To Kill a Mockingbird

Harper Lee

ॐ

Love will not serve those who do not live for her, and to whom she is not the breath of life.

The Ibsen Secret

Jennette Lee

ॐ

Are not all loves secretly the same? A hundred flowers sprung from a single root.

Delirium's Mistress

If you run away from trouble, it always follows.

Wolf Tower

Tanith Lee

ॐ

One voice speaking truth is greater force than fleets and armies.

The Left Hand of Darkness

Love doesn't just sit there, like a stone, it has to be made, like bread; remade all the time, made new.

The Lathe of Heaven

To see that your life is a story while you're in the middle of living it may be a help to living it well.

Gifts

Ursula K. Le Guin

∽

Anger is a signal, and one worth listening to.

The Dance of Anger

Fear is a message—sometimes helpful, sometimes not—but often conveying critical information about our beliefs, our needs, and our relationship to the world around us.

Fear and Other Uninvited Guests

Harriet Lerner

∽

I am not a victim. I am alive, wide awake and free from the numbness of apathy.

Daily Affirmations

Rokelle Lerner

∽

Spirituality is a brave search for the truth about existence, fearlessly peering into the mysterious nature of life.

The Seeker's Guide

Elizabeth Lesser

Laughter is by definition healthy.

The Summer Before Dark

Think wrongly, if you please, but in all cases think for yourself.

The Times newspaper

What's terrible is to pretend that the second-rate is first-rate. To pretend that you don't need love when you do; or you like your work when you know quite well you're capable of better.

The Golden Notebook

Doris Lessing

ട്ട

It is helpful to know the proper way to behave, so one can decide whether or not to be proper.

Ella Enchanted

There's nothing wrong with reading a book you love over and over. When you do, the words get inside you, become a part of you, in a way that words in a book you've read once can't.

Writing Magic

Gail Carson Levine

ട്ട

Family traditions counter alienation and confusion. They help us define who we are; they provide something steady, reliable and safe in a confusing world.

New Traditions

Susan Lieberman

Optimism works in conjunction with your life energy, strengthening your roots and keeping you grounded, stimulating the growth of new shoots and the development of new branches that form your life, energizing the creation that is you.

Power Optimism

Dana Lightman

৯

It is only in solitude that I ever find my own core.

Against Wind and Tide

To be deeply in love is, of course, a great liberating force.

Hour of Gold, Hour of Lead

It takes as much courage to have tried and failed as it does to have tried and succeeded.

Speak with Power and Grace
by Linda Swink

Anne Morrow Lindbergh

৯

I love being a woman . . . I love being sexy and feeling sexy. But the best thing about being a woman is the power we have over men.

Eva Longoria's Official Facebook Page

Eva Longoria

৯

I remain an eternal optimist about love. Sometimes it doesn't work, and that's sad. But I believe in love.

Shape magazine

I only do what my gut tells me to. I think it's smart to listen to other people's advice, but at the end of the day, you're the only one who can tell you what's right for you.

iVillage

I know it's hard for women to tap into that feeling of self-worth. We need to get the message out that you are valued, you are a goddess and don't forget that. It's about stopping those thoughts of negativity and insecurity.

Cosmopolitan, UK magazine

Jennifer Lopez

ॐ

Mistakes are part of the dues one pays for a full life.

The Ladies' Home Journal

There is a fountain of youth: it is your mind, your talents, the creativity you bring to your life, and the lives of people you love. When you learn to tap this source, you will have truly defeated age.

Reader's Digest magazine

Sophia Loren

ॐ

Being offended is part of being in the real world.

Spin magazine

I'm not a woman. I'm a force of nature.

The Biography Channel

Courtney Love

The deepest moments of intimacy occur when you're not talking.

O, The Oprah Magazine

The truth about love is that it is ever changing. Throughout the life of a relationship, individuals change and life itself changes. Love has to be flexible enough to accommodate new information, new roles, and new ways of loving one another.

The Truth About Love

Patricia Love

ೲ

Eat well, sleep and laugh. When you laugh, the lines go up instead of down.

O, The Oprah Magazine

Carey Lowell

ೲ

Love has pride in nothing—but its own humility.

The Women

Clare Boothe Luce

ೲ

A heart filled with anger has no room for love.

Wake-Up Calls

A positive attitude is something everyone can work on. And everyone can learn how to employ it.

Cable News Network

A fulfilling life is different to each person. You have to acknowledge your dreams, and not just wait for life to happen, and opportunities to come knocking at your door.

Cable News Network

Joan Lunden

ॐ

The power of one, if fearless and focused, is formidable, but the power of many working together is better.

Samuel Smiles' Self Help,
by Steve Shipside

Gloria Macapagal-Arroyo

ॐ

After all, life, for all its agonies of despair and loss and guilt, is exciting and beautiful, amusing and artful and endearing, full of liking and love, at times a poem and a high adventure, at times noble and at times very gay; and whatever (if anything) is to come after it—we shall not have this life again.

The Towers of Trebizond

Rose Macaulay

ॐ

It's not that optimism solves all of life's problems; it is just that it can sometimes make the difference between coping and collapsing.

Learn to Be an Optimist

Lucy MacDonald

In an age when everyone is constantly busy and short of time, what could be more enjoyable than taking time to indulge in what was once part of everyday life, but has now become a luxury—afternoon tea

The Book of Afternoon Tea

Lesley Mackley

ഛ

A person who knows how to laugh at himself will never cease to be amused.

Family Circle magazine

I don't need a man to rectify my existence. The most profound relationship we'll ever have is the one with ourselves.

New Woman magazine

The more I traveled the more I realized that our fear makes strangers of people who should be friends.

Don't Fall Off the Mountain

Shirley MacLaine

ഛ

Not all Freudian slips are created equal.

The Rachel Maddow Show

The downside of playing dumb is that you sound dumb.

The Rachel Maddow Show

Rachel Maddow

A lot of people are afraid to say what they want. That's why they don't get what they want.

Sex

Madonna

❦

I always felt that the great high privilege, relief and comfort of friendship was that one had to explain nothing.

The Collected Letters of Katherine Mansfield

When we can begin to take our failures nonseriously, it means we are ceasing to be afraid of them. It is of immense importance to learn to laugh at ourselves.

The Journal of Katherine Mansfield

Katherine Mansfield

❦

The things you think are the disasters in your life are not the disasters really. Almost anything can be turned around: out of every ditch, a path, if you can only see it.

Bring Up the Bodies

Hilary Mantel

❦

Humans have long since possessed the tools for crafting a better world. Where love, compassion, altruism and justice have failed, genetic manipulation will not succeed.

Quest for Perfection

Gina Maranto

A caress is better than a career.

Careers for Women

Elisabeth Marbury

∾

You can live a lifetime and, at the end of it, know more about other people than you know about yourself.

West with the Night

Beryl Markham

∾

Self-esteem is the real magic wand that can form a child's future. A child's self-esteem affects every area of her existence, from friends she chooses, to how well she does academically in school, to what kind of job she gets, to even the person she chooses to marry.

The Magic of Encouragement

Stephanie Marston

∾

In the best of all possible worlds, childbirth enriches a marriage. In the worst, it harms it. No matter how good their marriage is, most couples find that having a baby challenges their relationship.

Your Maternity Leave

Jean Marzollo

∾

You'll never regret writing any letter out of love. It's a good idea to reread anything you've written in anger.

Letters to My Daughters

Mary Matalin

What is death? Death is the ending of life . . . The truth is, nothing can live forever. Everyone and everything will die in time. Plants, animals, and people all die. Death is a natural part of life.

Death

Joanne Mattern

୬

I always did something I was a little not ready to do. I think that's how you grow. When there's that moment of 'Wow, I'm not really sure I can do this,' and you push through those moments, that's when you have a break through.

Marissa Mayer speech:
Six Life Lessons from Yahoo CEO

Marissa Mayer

୬

You can have anything you want if you make up your mind and you want it.

I Dream a World by Brian Lanker

Clara McBride-Hale

୬

Our destinies are the culmination of all the choices we've made along the way, which is why it's imperative to listen hard to your inner voice when it speaks up. Don't let anyone else's noise drown it out

The Complete Jessica Darling Series

Megan McCafferty

Make no judgements where you have no compassion.

The Dragonriders of Pern

Anne McCaffrey

ॐ

What's the use of falling in love if you both remain inertly as you were?

Between Friends

You mustn't force sex to do the work of love, or love to do the work of sex.

The Group

To be disesteemed by people you don't have much respect for is not the worst fate.

The New York Times

Mary McCarthy

ॐ

I was just so interested in what I was doing I could hardly wait to get up in the morning and get at it.

A Feeling for the Organism,
by Evelyn Fox Keller

If you know you're right, you don't care. You know that sooner or later, it will come out in the wash.

Interview by Claudia Wellis,
Time magazine

Barbara McClintock

The only courage that matters is the kind that gets you from one minute to the next.

The Complete Neurotic's Notebook

Mignon McLaughlin

§

Don't sabotage your own greatness by succumbing to failure.

A Day Late and a Dollar Short

Too many of us are hung up on what we don't have, can't have, or won't ever have. We spend too much energy being down, when we could use that same energy—if not less of it—doing, or at least trying to do, some of the things we really want to do.

Disappearing Acts

Terry McMillan

§

Never doubt that a small group of thoughtful, committed citizens can change the world: indeed, it's the only thing that ever has.

Curing Nuclear Madness
by Frank Somers and Tana Dineen

We are living beyond our means. As a people we have developed a life-style that is draining the earth of its priceless and irreplaceable resources without regard for the future of our children and people all around the world.

Progress as if Survival Mattered by Hugh Nash

Margaret Mead

Those who do not know how to weep with their whole heart don't know how to laugh either.

Ms. magazine

Golda Meir

ى

Science makes people reach selflessly for truth and objectivity; it teaches people to accept reality, with wonder and admiration, not to mention the deep awe and joy that the natural order of things brings to the true scientist.

Lecture, Austrian UNESCO Commission

Lise Meitner

ى

There is one red line that we should not cross. It is a commitment to human rights, the respect of the dignity of the human being. There should be no compromises.

The New York Times

Angela Merkel

ى

I didn't belong as a kid, and that always bothered me. If only I'd known that one day differentness would be an asset, then my early life would have been much easier.

Woman's Day magazine

Bette Midler

My motto is that each and every one of us can make a difference, but together we make change.

Mikulski.senate.gov

The women of the Senate are like the U.S. Olympic team: we come in different sizes, but we sure are united in our determination to do the best for our country!

Democratic National Convention speech

Barbara A. Mikulski

৯

Not truth, but faith, it is that keeps the world alive.

Renascence and Other Poems

Edna St. Vincent Millay

৯

Fulfillment derives not from lofty achievements, but from ordinary feats. It arrives not once in a lifetime, but every moment of the livelong day.

Hand Wash Cold

Karen Maezen Miller

৯

To love is simply to allow another to be, live, grow, expand, become. An appreciation that demands and expects nothing in return.

Sita

Kate Millet

Reality is something you rise above.

Interview with Rona Barrett

Liza Minnelli

❧

An unhappy mother does not raise a happy child.

JoniMitchell.com

Joni Mitchell

❧

Life's under no obligation to give us what we expect. We take what we get and are thankful it's no worse than it is.

Gone with the Wind

Margaret Mitchell

❧

For loneliness is but cutting adrift from our moorings and floating out to sea; an opportunity for finding ourselves, our real selves, what we are about, where we are heading during our little time on this beautiful earth.

Singing in the Rain

Anne Shannon Monroe

❧

Happiness never becomes a habit.

My Story

We are all born sexual creatures, thank God, but it's a pity so many people despise and crush the natural gift. Art, real art, comes from it, everything.

Life magazine

Marilyn Monroe

ॐ

Children are human beings to whom respect is due, superior to us by reason of their innocence and of the greater possibilities of their future.

Daily Montessori.com

Of all things love is the most potent.

Daily Montessori.com

Maria Montessori

ॐ

I love to smell flowers in the dark . . . You get hold of their soul.

Anne of Green Gables

We pay a price for everything we get or take in this world, and although ambitions are well worth having, they are not to be cheaply won, but exact their dues of work and self-denial, anxiety and discouragement.

Anne of Green Gables

Lucy Maud Montgomery

I think there is no way to reach your fullest potential if you don't really find the love of yourself.

Harper's Bazaar

Demi Moore

ᘛ

Generosity is giving what you could use yourself.

The Complete Prose of Marianne Moore

Marianne Moore

ᘛ

The belief that love is a finite essence that will eventually run out holds a certain logic for me even now, even if I am supposed to know better.

The Big Girls

Susanna Moore

ᘛ

Age does not protect you from love. But love, to some extent, protects you from age.

La Moreau by Marianne Gray

Jeanne Moreau

ᘛ

Magic is not a practice. It is a living, breathing web of energy that, with our permission can encase our every action.

Everyday Magic

Dorothy Morrison

Make a difference about something other than yourselves.

Song of Solomon

If there's a book you really want to read but it hasn't been written yet, then you must write it.

Toni Morrison
by Corinne Naden and Rose Blue

Two parents can't raise a child any more than one. You need a whole community—everybody—to raise a child.

Time magazine

Oppressive language does more than represent violence; it is violence; does more than represent the limits of knowledge; it limits knowledge.

Nobel Lecture

Toni Morrison

ɕ

Until you make peace with who you are, you'll never be content with what you have.

The Huffington Post

Doris Mortman

ɕ

I rejected the notion that my race or sex would bar my success in life.

Equal Justice Under Law:
An Autobiography

Something which we think is impossible now is not impossible in another decade.

I Dream a World by Brian Lanker

Constance Baker Motley

❧

God gave us relatives, thank God we can choose our friends.

The Complete Cynic's Calendar

Ethel Watts Mumford

❧

The constant happiness is curiosity.

Writers & Company
by Eleanor Wachtel

Alice Munro

❧

When you don't talk, there's a lot of stuff that ends up not getting said.

Dairy Queen

Catherine Gilbert Murdock

❧

We can only learn to love by loving.

Understanding Iris Murdock

Iris Murdoch

Isn't it amazing how the people who know the least throw the biggest stones?

Twitter post, Feb. 28, 2012

People see me as the girl next door, everything came easy, and that was not the case. It was hard, hard work and a lot of bumps along the way.

Mansbridge One on One interview

Anne Murray

ૐ

I understand the importance of community, clubs and everyone getting together to make a fun environment for kids and adults to thrive in.

Cable News Network

We have loads of talented kids. It's not about talent, it's about the opportunity. Talent without opportunity is nothing.

The Scotsman

Judy Murray

ૐ

I think often young people, particularly young women, don't see [being a senator] as a career or something they can do. If I plant the seeds, someday the US Senate will be half women.

"When I was a Girl, Patty Murray Told Me to Run for Office,"
Anna Minard, *The Stranger* (Seattle newspaper)

Patty Murray

Do you really want to look back on your life and see how wonderful it could have been had you not been afraid to live it? Choice is the process of creation itself.

Anatomy of the Spirit

You have resources yet to be unleashed. Make bold, courageous choices. Live as though you have the power to change the world—because you do.

Defy Gravity

Caroline Myss

༉

When we engage in what we are naturally suited to do, our work takes on the quality of play and it is play that stimulates creativity.

Brains Inventing Themselves,
by Conrad P. Pritscher

Linda Naiman

༉

Fear of the unknown translates to fear of losing control. In order to feel safe, we feel we must control every variable. Controlling everything that's around the corner simply isn't possible.

Speak Without Fear

Ivy Naistadt

༉

I think the key is for women not to set any limits.

Ladies' Home Journal

Martina Navratilova

The family is both the fundamental unit of society as well as the root of culture. It . . . is a perpetual source of encouragement, advocacy, assurance, and emotional refueling that empowers a child to venture with confidence into the greater world and to become all that he can be.

Dr. Mom's Parenting Guide

Marianne E. Neifert

ς∾

True strength is delicate.

Women's Realities, Women's Choices,
by Hunter College Women's Studies Collective

The freer that women become, the freer men will be. Because when you enslave someone, you are enslaved.

The Biography Channel

Louise Nevelson

ς∾

Passion gives me moments of wholeness.

The Diary of Anais Nin

Life shrinks or expands in proportion to one's courage.

The Diary of Anais Nin

To withhold from living is to die . . . the more you give of your-self to life the more life nourishes you.

Fire

Each friend represents a world in us, a world possibly not born until they arrive, and it is only by this meeting that a new world is born.

New Woman magazine

I, with a deeper instinct, choose a man who compels my strength, who makes enormous demands on me, who does not doubt my courage or my toughness, who does not believe me naïve or innocent, who has the courage to treat me like a woman.

Henry and June

Anais Nin

൸

Only love heals. Anger, guilt, and fear can only destroy.

Evermore

The best way to deal with eternity is by living it one day at a time.

Evermore

Fear separates—makes us feel alone—disconnected—while love—love does just the opposite—it unties.

Shadowland

Alyson Noel

൸

The future of the world rests with women.

YouTube, PepsiCo CEO

Take a stand. Be known for your courage and confidence.

The Women's Conference

If there is (a glass ceiling), remember it is made of glass and it can be easily broken. All you have to do is try.

Interview by Ranjani Saigal

I am not sure I have been the best at doing the work family balance. I think there are no right answers to that question. It is a constant struggle. I am very fortunate to have support from both sides of my family. My husband has been incredibly supportive.

Interview by Ranjani Saigal

Indra Krishnamurthy Nooyi

ॐ

Knowing is the most profound kind of love, giving someone the gift of knowledge about yourself.

Taking Center Stage by Janet Brown

Marsha Norman

ॐ

Life is easier than you'd think; all that is necessary is to accept the impossible, do without the indispensable and bear the intolerable.

Today's Health magazine

Kathleen Norris

ॐ

True health is only possible when we understand the unity of our minds, emotions, spirits, and physical bodies.

DrNorthrup.com

When we find the connection between our thoughts, beliefs, physical health, and life circumstances, we find that we are in the driver's seat of our lives and can make profound changes. Nothing is more exhilarating or empowering.

DrNorthrup.com

Christiane Northrup

ೲ

Success doesn't count unless you earn it fair and square.

Democratic National Convention speech

As women, we must stand up for ourselves. As women, we must stand up for each other. As women, we must stand up for justice for all.

The Biography Channel

One of the lessons that I grew up with was to always stay true to yourself and never let what somebody else says distract you from your goals.

Marie Claire magazine

We should always have three friends in our lives—one who walks ahead who we look up to and we follow; one who walks beside us, who is with us every step of our journey; and then, one who we reach back for and we bring along after we've cleared the way.

National Mentoring Summit

Michelle Obama

ೲ

I don't know that there are any shortcuts to doing a good job.

Sandra Day O'Connor by Ann McFeatters

Young women today often have very little appreciation for the real battles that took place to get women where they are today in this country. I don't know how much history young women today know about those battles.

Sandra Day O'Conner by Dennis Abrams

Sandra Day O'Connor

༝

Love cannot survive if you just give it scraps of yourself, scraps of your time, scraps of your thoughts.

Something More by Sarah Ban Breathnach

Mary O'Hara

༝

I feel there is something unexplored about women that only a woman can explore . . .

An Enduring Spirit by Katherine Hoffman

Georgia O'Keeffe

༝

I am a woman above everything else.

Jacqueline Kennedy Onassis,
by David Lestor

One must not let oneself be overwhelmed by sadness.

The Uncommon Wisdom of
Jacqueline Kennedy Onassis

There are many little ways to enlarge your child's world. Love of books is the best of all.

Matchbook magazine by Katie Armour

Jackie Kennedy Onassis

Maybe that was the secret of happiness—not expecting any one thing to last forever.

The Lost Recipe for Happiness

Barbara O'Neal

෨

While women may fake orgasms, men fake finances.

Oprah.com:12 Priceless Money
Lessons from Suze Orman

Thoughtful financial planning can easily take a backseat to daily life.

O, The Oprah Magazine

When you are grateful—when you can see what you have— you unlock blessings to flow in your life.

Suze Orman's Recession Rescue Plan

Suze Orman

෨

When you connect with them, people want to help you . . . When we really see each other, we want to help each other.

Ted Talks, Amanda Palmer: The Art of Asking

We can only connect the dots that we collect . . . Your connections are the thread that you weave into the cloth that becomes the story that only you can tell.

Interview by Maria Popova

Amanda Palmer

The upside to grief is it takes away your appetite. When people say you look good they really mean it. Nature's thoughtful that way.

Mick Harte Was Here

Barbara Park

Ϩ

Brevity is the soul of lingerie.

Not Much Fun

Dorothy Parker

Ϩ

As a woman, I have an inherent need to be all things to all people, to make certain everybody's taken care of. I know I can't sustain that level all the time, so I'm finding the proper balance and it's made me infinitely happier.

Woman's Day magazine

Sarah Jessica Parker

Ϩ

Each person must live their life as a model for others.

The Biography Channel

I have learned over the years that when one's mind is made up, this diminishes fear, knowing what must be done does away with fear.

The Biography Channel

The advice I would give to any young person is, first of all, to rid themselves of prejudice against other people and to be concerned about what they can do to help others.

Interview, achievement .org

Rosa Parks

❧

Marriage is, in actual fact, just a way of living. Before marriage, we don't expect life to be all sunshine and roses, but we seem to expect marriage to be that way.

Saving Your Marriage Before It Starts

Leslie L. Parrott

❧

The way I see it, if you want the rainbow, you gotta put up with the rain.

This is Not the Life I Ordered

Dolly Parton

❧

Never be so focused on what you're looking for that you overlook the thing you actually find.

State of Wonder

Shame should be reserved for the things we choose to do, not the circumstances that life puts on us.

Truth and Beauty

If you're trying to find out what's coming next, turn off everything you own that has an off switch and listen.

What Now?

It was never the right time or it was always the right time, depending on how you looked at it.

Bel Canto

Ann Patchett

৯

Women are fifty percent of our population and there is simply no way our nation can progress if its population is left behind.

The Hindu

Women have talent and intelligence but, due to social constraints and prejudices, it is still a long distance away from the goal of gender equality.

The Weekly Voice

Pratibha Patil

৯

There will never be a new world order until women are a part of it.

American Heroes, Salem Press

I always feel . . . the movement is a sort of mosaic. Each of us puts in one little stone, and then you get a great mosaic at the end.

Historical Viewpoints by John A. Garraty

Alice Paul

No one can arrive from being talented alone. God gives talent, work transforms talent into genius.

The Biography Channel

Anna Pavlova

❦

Depression is a treatable medical illness like cancer and heart disease.

Depression

Judith Peacock

❦

Women are leaders everywhere you look—from the CEO who runs a Fortune 500 company to the housewife who raises her children and heads her household. Our country was built by strong women and we will continue to break down walls and defy stereotypes.

Glamour magazine

Nancy Pelosi

❦

The ultimate test of a relationship is to disagree but to hold hands.

How to Make Love to a Man

Alexandra Penney

❦

Being a woman has only bothered me in climbing trees.

Time magazine

Most of man's problems upon this planet, in the long history of the race, have been met and solved either partially or as a whole by experiment based on common sense and carried out with courage.

People at Work

Frances Perkins

ဢ

I am my own woman.

The Biography Channel

I demanded more rights for women because I know what women had to put up with.

The Biography Channel

Eva Peron

ဢ

There was a lot of the word, no, being sent my way, and I never accepted that.

The Ellen DeGeneres Show

I think it's important to start breaking down the idea that to achieve your dream you always have to be perfect or flawless or live in some kind of fantasy world.

The Ellen DeGeneres Show

I've learnt I'm in a very modern fairytale, but I also know I don't need the Prince Charming to have a happy ending. I can make the happy ending myself.

Daily Record

Katy Perry

If you have made mistakes, even serious ones, there is always another chance for you. What we call failure is not the falling down, but the staying down.

*Glamou*r magazine

Mary Pickford

ॐ

Shared laughter is erotic too.

Sex Wars

I think we validate our lives through our actions.

The Writer's Chronicle

If you want to be listened to, you should put in time listening.

O, The Oprah Magazine

Marge Piercy

ॐ

If you expect nothing from anybody, you're never disappointed.

The Bell Jar

I have the choice of being constantly active and happy or introspectively passive and sad. Or I can go mad by ricocheting in between.

The Unabridged Journals of Sylvia Plath

Sylvia Plath

The real winners in life are the people who look at every situation with an expectation that they can make it work or make it work better.

The Walk Out Woman

Barbara Pletcher

❧

When men are oppressed, it's a tragedy. When women are oppressed, it's tradition.

Deborah, Golda, and Me

Letty Cottin Pogrebin

❧

Like Broadway, the novel, and God, feminism has been declared dead many times.

Reasonable Creatures

Katha Pollitt

❧

The influence of a beautiful, helpful, hopeful character is contagious . . . People radiate what is in their minds and in their hearts.

Pollyanna

Eleanor H. Porter

❧

Love must be learned, and learned again and again; there is no end to it.

The Days Before

Trust your happiness and richness of your life at this moment. It is as true and as much yours as anything that ever happened to you.

Letters of Katherine Anne Porter

There are so many things we are capable of, that we could be or do. The potentialities are so great that we never, any of us, are more than one-fourth fulfilled.

The Paris Review

Katherine Anne Porter

❧

Manners are a sensitive awareness of the feelings of others. If you have that awareness, you have good manners, no matter what fork you use.

EmilyPost.com

Emily Post

❧

What we are is God's gift to us. What we become is our gift to God.

People Will Talk by John Kobal

Eleanor Powell

❧

You do a lot of things, sometimes, before you can decide what you want to do.

I Dream a World by Brian Lanker

Georgia Davis Powers

Unfortunately, sometimes people don't hear you until you scream.

People magazine

Stefanie Powers

ℒ

Accomplishments have no color.

The Biography Channel

You should always know when you're shifting gears in life. You should leave your era, it should never leave you.

I Dream a World by Brian Lanker

Leontyne Price

ℒ

Truth travels slowly when rumors have wings of gold.

Boneshaker

Ideas come from everywhere. New ideas are never the problem; finding the time to act on them—that's the problem.

Alternative Magazine Online

Cherie Priest

ℒ

The world is round and the place which may seem like the end, may also be only the beginning.

Parade

Ivy Baker Priest

It was the outstretched hands, the giving, that mattered.

The Shipping News

E. Annie Proulx

ᔿ

The fashionable woman wears clothes. The clothes don't wear her.

Marie Claire magazine

Fashion is a tool . . . to compete in life outside the home. People like you better, without knowing why, because people always react well to a person they like the looks of.

Quant by Quant

Mary Quant

ᔿ

Don't ever confuse—your life and your work. The second is only part of the first.

A Short Guide to a Happy Life

The thing that is really hard, and really amazing, is giving up on being perfect and beginning the work of becoming yourself.

Being Perfect

If men got pregnant, there would be safe, reliable methods of birth control. They'd be inexpensive, too.

Living Out Loud

Look back, to slavery, to suffrage, to integration and one thing
is clear. Fashions in bigotry come and go. The right thing lasts.

The New York Times

Anna Quindlen

ॐ

Begin each day as if it were on purpose.

Lean Forward into Your Life

There is no small act of kindness. Every compassionate act
makes large the world.

Live Boldly

Courage doesn't always roar. Sometimes courage is the quiet
voice at the end of the day saying, "I will try again tomorrow."

Simply an Inspired Life

Mary Anne Radmacher

ॐ

Retirement is not a static event, fixed in time with a gold watch
to mark it. Rather retirement—if that is even the right word—
is a multidirectional process that can take many years.

Women Confronting Retirement

Alice Radosh

ॐ

The man who does not value himself, cannot value anything
or anyone.

The Virtue of Selfishness

Happiness is the state of consciousness which proceeds from the achievement of one's values.

Atlas Shrugged

My happiness is not the means to any end. It is the end. It is its own goal. It is its own purpose.

Anthem

Ayn Rand

ᘯ

It's hubris to think that the way we see things is everything there is.

Discover magazine

Speculation and the exploration of ideas beyond what we know with certainty are what leads to progress.

The New York Times

When people try to use religion to address the natural world, science pushes back on it, and religion has to accommodate the results. Beliefs can be permanent, but beliefs can also be flexible. Personally, if I find out my belief is wrong, I change my mind. I think that's a good way to live.

Discover magazine

Lisa Randall

ᘯ

A strong woman understands that the gifts such as logic, decisiveness, and strength are just as feminine as intuition and emotional connection. She values and uses all of her gifts.

Psychology Today magazine

Nancy Rathburn

Food was always a conduit in our family for storytelling, and it was a way for us to keep in touch and remember things. We're people that use food to keep each other together and to always cheer us up and make all of our days better.

Newsweek magazine

Rachael Ray

ക

A man in love…is the master, so it seems, but only if his lady friend permits it! The need to interchange the roles of slave and master for the sake of the relationship is never more clearly demonstrated than in the course of an affair.

The Secret Record by Maxwell Perkins

Pauline Reage (Dominique Aury)

ക

Integrity is so perishable in the summer months of success.

Good-bye Baby and Amen by David Bailey

Vanessa Redgrave

ക

It is important to take every experience as a learning opportunity.

Bill Good interview at the
Beedie School of Business.

When educating the minds of our youth, we must not forget to educate their hearts.

At the Status of Women Committee on
Prospects for Canadian Girls

Tracy Redies

We cannot really love anybody with whom we never laugh.

The Love List by Leslie L. Parrot

It is not easy to find happiness in ourselves, and it is not possible to find it elsewhere.

Women and Leadership by Genevieve Brown

Agnes Repplier

ൟ

What we like about women is sensuality, wildness, hormones. Women who make a song and dance about their intuition.

The God of Carnage

Yasmina Reza

ൟ

You do have a story inside you; it lies articulate and waiting to be written—behind your silence and your suffering.

Pandora

Anne Rice

ൟ

The moment of change is the only poem.

Adrienne Rich by Cheri Colby Langdell

All human life on the planet is born of woman.

Introduction from *Of Woman Born*
by Andrea O'Reilly

It's exhilarating to be alive in a time of awakening consciousness; it can also be confusing, disorienting, and painful.

A Woman's Place by Shirley Morahan

The connections between and among women are the most feared the most problematic, and the most potentially transforming force on the planet.

A Promise and a Way of Life,
by Becky W. Thompson

Adrienne Rich

૭

It takes a couple of years just to get the background and knowledge that you need before you can go into detailed training for your mission.

Scholastic, interview by students

Sally Ride

૭

There are as many ways to survive as there are survivors.

Good Housekeeping magazine

Amanda Robb

૭

The older you get, the more fragile you understand life to be. I think that's good motivation for getting out of bed joyfully each day.

Daily Mail

Julia Roberts

I've found out that falling in love doesn't have anything to do with time. It can take a year or an instant, It happens when it's ready to happen.

The Calhouns

If you don't go after what you want, you'll never have it. If you don't ask, the answer's always no. If you don't step forward, you're always in the same place.

Tears of the Moon

Create that good, solid foundation, and the man who comes into your life can be that delicious icing.

inReads interview

Nora Roberts

☙

There is no magical reason why I am where I am. And there is absolutely no reason why you can't be where you want to be. If it can happen for me, it can happen for you, too. And it would be a privilege for me to help you get there.

From the Heart

You want to say, "Everything's the same; I'm living with cancer and it's not going to stop me. But until you really test yourself and challenge yourself, I don't think you quite know."

People magazine

Robin Roberts

☙

I tell young people to believe in themselves, particularly young women, and to have confidence.

Interview by Sheila Langan

I wanted to share my own experience and very much to encourage others to believe that not only does everybody matter, but everybody can make a difference.

Interview by Sheila Langan

Mary Robinson

੬

The individual can make a difference.

I Dream a World by Brian Lanker

Rachel Robinson

੬

Whatever you do, be different—that was the advice my mother gave me, and I can't think of better advice for an entrepreneur. If you're different, you will stand out.

The Body Shop, Founder

Anita Roddick

੬

The most important thing in anyone's life is to be giving something.

GingerRogers.com

When two people love each other, they don't look at each other, they look in the same direction.

GingerRogers.com

Ginger Rogers

੬

Don't let others define you. You define yourself.

Fortune magazine

I learned to always take on things I'd never done before.

Financial News Network

Someone once told me growth and comfort do not coexist. And I think it's a really good thing to remember.

Fortune's Most Powerful Women Summit

Virginia "Ginni" Rometty

ॐ

The giving of love is an education in itself.

Eleanor Roosevelt,
by Blanche Wiesen Cook

When you cease to make a contribution you begin to die.

You Learn by Living

Life was meant to be lived, and curiosity must be kept alive.

Autobiography

No one can make you feel inferior without your consent.

This is My Story

It is not fair to ask of others what you are not willing to do yourself.

My Day, newspaper column

The future belongs to those who believe in the beauty of their dreams.

It Seems to Me

It isn't enough to talk about peace. One must believe in it. And it isn't enough to believe in it. One must work at it.

Voice of America radio broadcast
Eleanor Roosevelt

ॐ

People vote with their hearts, not their heads.

The Wall Street Journal

First, make a difference . . . Second, take some risks—prudent risks, of course! Third, seek out mentors . . . Fourth, ask for what you want.

Forbes magazine

Endorphins are a very powerful thing. Sports have always been a really important part of how I energizer myself, as well as how I relax.

Forbes magazine

How you manage change can make all the difference. During our transformation, we put a premium on communication from day one. We also made a point of celebrating success . . . publicly and often.

The Wall Street Journal
Irene Rosenfeld

ॐ

Life consists of two sides . . . light and dark. Joy and sorrow. Without a balance, one cannot fully experience a full and well-rounded life.

No Safe Place
JoAnn Ross

Our work is not to change what you do, but to witness what you do with enough awareness, enough curiosity, enough tenderness.

Official Facebook page

Geneen Roth

❧

I hope the fathers and mothers of little girls will look at them and say 'yes, women can.'

Cable News Network

Dilma Rousseff

❧

When you see what some girls marry, you realize how they must hate to work for a living.

A Guide to Men

Never worry for fear you have broken a man's heart; at the worst it is only sprained and a week's rest will put it in perfect working condition again.

A Guide to Men

Helen Rowland

❧

It takes a great deal of courage to stand up to your enemies, but even more to stand up to your friends.

Harry Potter and the Sorcerer's Stone

I have never been remotely ashamed of having been depressed. Never. What's to be ashamed of? I went through a really rough time and I am quite proud that I got out of that.

USA Today

We do not need magic to change the world. We carry all the power we need inside ourselves already: we have the power to imagine better.

Harvard Alumni Association speech

J. K. Rowling

࿐

In hindsight, my initial love for fashion was about hope and evolving to become the type of woman I wanted to be: strong, confident and feminine.

Newsweek magazine

Rachel Roy

࿐

Sometimes it takes years to really grasp what has happened to your life.

I Dream a World by Brian Lanker

Wilma Rudolph

࿐

I didn't want to be a boy, ever, but I was outraged that his height and intelligence were graces for him and gaucheries for me.

Lesbian Images: Essays

Jane Rule

࿐

Only by learning to love one another can our world be saved. Only love can conquer all.

Challenge to the Cold War

Dora Russell

Taking joy in life is a woman's best cosmetic.

Something More,
by Sarah Ban Breathnach

I'll match my flops with anybody's but I wouldn't have missed 'em. Flops are a part of life's menu and I've never been a girl to miss out on any of the courses.

Life is a Banquet

Rosalind Russell

∽

Oh, I'm so inadequate—and I love myself.

Wake-up Calls by Joan Lunden

Meg Ryan

∽

Being a good and fair person is very important in life.

CNN International

This is the century of us, this is the century of woman. Not every woman has got what I have. So if I could do something to help them that should also be my duty.

CNN International

Guler Sabanci

∽

The more one gardens, the more one learns, the more one realizes how little one knows. I suppose the whole of life is like that.

A Joy of Gardening

Women, like men, ought to have their years so glutted with freedom that they hate the very idea of freedom.

Harold and Vita by Nigel Nicolson

I have come to the conclusion, after many years of sometimes sad experience, that you cannot come to any conclusion at all.

In Your Garden Again

Vita Sackville-West

❧

I see dance being used as a means of communication between soul and soul, to express what is too deep to find for words.

Process in the Arts Therapies,
by Ann Cattanach

Ruth St. Denis

❧

There is only one happiness in life, to love and be loved.

Encyclopedia Britannica

Guard well within yourself that treasure, kindness. Know how to give without hesitation, how to lose without regret, how to acquire without meanness.

The Wooster Reader, Vol. 2 by Lizzie E. Wooster

Let us accept truth, even when it surprises us and alters our views.

Letters of George Sand

George Sand (Amantine Lucile Aurore Dupin)

The most important thing—and I've said it a hundred times and I'll say it a hundred times—if you marry a man, marry the right one.

The Huffington Post, YouTube

I feel really grateful to the people who encouraged me and helped me develop. Nobody can succeed on their own.

Lean In

I'm a feminist because I believe in women . . . it's a heavy word, feminism, but it's not one I think we should run from. I'm proud to be a feminist.

Lean In

Sheryl Sandberg

৯৯

Birth control is the first important step woman must take toward the goal of her freedom. It is the first step she must take to be man's equal. It is the first step they must both take toward human emancipation.

Birth Control Review

Woman must not accept; she must challenge. She must not be told how to use her freedom; she must find out for herself. She must not be awed by that which has been built up around her; she must reverence that within her which struggles for expression.

Birth Control Review

Margaret Sanger

True feelings justifies whatever cost.

Journal of a Solitude

Loneliness is the poverty of self; solitude is the richness of self.

Mrs. Stevens Hears the Mermaids Singing

Each day, and the living of it, has to be a conscious creation in which discipline and order are relieved with some play and pure foolishness.

Journal of a Solitude

May Sarton

ൟ

I'm always fascinated by the way memory diffuses fact.

TV Guide

Diane Sawyer

ൟ

The only sin passion can commit is to be joyless.

Gaudy Night

If we want a thing badly enough, we make it happen. If we let ourselves be discouraged, that is proof that our wanting was inadequate.

Begin Here: A Statement of Faith

Dorothy Sayers

ൟ

Parents aren't sex education experts just because they are parents.

Ten Talks Parents Must Have with Their Children

Pepper Schwartz

The critical responsibility for the generation you're in is, to help provide the shoulders, the direction, and the support for those generations who come behind.

National Geographic

Gloria Dean Randle Scott

ഏ

I think that women as a group are so powerful . . . I wish that we could come together more as a political force. If women ran the world, I don't believe that there would be war. I really don't . . . We understand the bigger picture. We understand our impact on the environment, on the world. We understand the generation that will go after us because we gave birth to them.

Newsweek magazine

Kyra Sedgwick

ഏ

I am never afraid of what I know.

Black Beauty

Anna Sewell

ഏ

I just want to be as healthy as I can for as long as I can.

Closer Weekly Magazine

I know that the purpose of life is to understand and be in the present moment with the people you love. It's just that simple.

The Mail interview by Cassie Carpenter

Jane Seymour

We can say "peace on Earth," we can sing about it, preach about it, or pray about it, but if we have not internalized the mythology to make it happen inside of us, then it will not be.

I Dream a World by Brian Lanker

Betty Shabazz

ॐ

We're only going to be able to compete in the world if we continue to be innovative.

Hosting a town hall forum in New Hampshire

Jeanne Shaheen

ॐ

The leaders are lacking love, and love is lacking leaders.

The Biography Channel

You can't achieve anything in life without a small amount of sacrifice.

Official Twitter account

My brain, I believe, is the most beautiful part of my body. Never stop learning, never stop seeking knowledge. Intelligence is your sexiest asset.

The Biography Channel

Shakira

In times past, honeymoons may have lasted longer and involved little expense, the outside world was more definitely shut out, and the partners devoted their attention to each other. Restoring this practice might help get marriages off to a better start by supporting partners' development of a secure couple bond and a strong boundary around their relationship.

The Ways We Love

Sheila A. Sharpe

ᔆ

To be somebody, a woman does not have to be more like a man, but has to be more of a woman.

The Ottawa Journal

Sally E. Shaywitz

ᔆ

If we don't change, we don't grow. If we don't grow, we are not really living. Growth demands a temporary surrender of security.

Passages

Gail Sheehy

ᔆ

Friendship is a serious affection; the most sublime of all affections, because it is founded on principle, and cemented by time.

A Vindication of the Rights of Women

Mary Wollstonecraft Shelley

Some of our early job experiences are like dating—it helps you figure out what you don't like.

The Globe and Mail

Karen Sheriff

ϣ

I always dream the best case scenario and accept it if it doesn't happen.

NBC Sports

Mikaela Shiffrin

ϣ

When you forgive, you heal your own anger and hurt and are able to let love lead again. It's like spring cleaning for your heart.

Happy for No Reason

Marci Shimoff

ϣ

Trouble is a part of life, and if you don't share it, you don't give the person who loves you a chance to love you enough.

Dinah! by Bruce Cassiday

Dinah Shore

ϣ

When the world is so complicated, the simple gift of friendship is within all of our hands.

People.com

The gift my mother gave me was the gift of possibility. From an early age, she instilled in me a belief that I could do anything I wanted to do.

Today, NBC News

Women somehow get portrayed as one type. You're either a feminist or you're not. You're a working woman or you're not. I'm raising two girls, and I say to them, "I need you to be strong and soft. You can be smart and beautiful . . . You can be all of these things."

Women's Media Center interview by Marianne Schnall

Maria Shriver

༖

Chains do not hold a marriage together. It is threads, hundreds of tiny threads which sew people together through the years.

Daily Mail

Simone Signoret

༖

There are no shortcuts to any place worth going.

The Biography Channel

You may be disappointed if you fail, but you are doomed if you don't try.

"Having It All," essay

There is a growing strength in women but it's in the forehead not the forearm.

Time magazine

Beverly Sills

∽

If your dreams do not scare you, they are not big enough.

This Child Will Be Great

Women work harder. And women are more honest; they have less reasons to be corrupt.

The New York Times

Ellen Johnson Sirleaf

∽

Confidence is you've been on that bull before and you know you're gonna ride 'em.

Letters to a Young Artist

Anna Deavere Smith

∽

Lack of confidence is what makes you want to change somebody else's mind. When you're OK, you don't need to convince anyone else in order to empower yourself.

Good Housekeeping magazine

Jada Pinkett Smith

∽

I had no proof that I had the stuff to be an artist, though I hungered to be one.

Just Kids

Never let go of that fiery sadness called desire.

Elle magazine

Please, no matter how we advance technologically, please don't abandon the book. There is nothing in our material world more beautiful than the book.

National Book Awards speech

Patti Smith

&

"Woman" is my slave name; feminism will give me freedom to seek some other identity altogether.

Conflicts in Feminism

Ann Snitow

&

Hope just means another world might be possible, not promised, not quarantined. Hope calls for action; action is impossible without hope.

Hope in the Dark

Rebecca Solnit

&

Ambition if it feeds at all, does so on the ambition of others.

The Benefactor

The only interesting answers are those which destroy the questions.

The Benefactor

What is most beautiful in virile men is something feminine; what is most beautiful in feminine women is something masculine.

The Partisan Review

Susan Sontag

ତ

I have never, ever focused on the negative of things, I always look at the positive.

National Public Radio

Although I grew up in a modest and challenging circumstances, I consider my life to be immeasurably rich.

The Biography Channel

Sonia Sotomayor

ତ

I see no reason to keep silent about my enjoyment of the sound of my own voice.

Loitering with Intent

Muriel Spark

ତ

When you're comfortable with someone you love, the silence is the best.

Elle magazine

Every night, I have to read a book, so that my mind will stop thinking about things that I stress about.

People magazine

Britney Spears

The human mind always makes progress, but it is a progress in spirals.

Ms. magazine

Madame de Stael

༙

The best protection any woman can have . . . is courage.

History of Woman Suffrage

Women's discontent increase in exact proportion to her development.

History of Woman Suffrage

We hold these truths to be self-evident, that all men and women are created equal . . .

Declaration of Rights and Sentiments

Elizabeth Cady Stanton

༙

You are always the same age inside.

The American Treasury

Let me listen to me and not to them.

Stanzas in Meditation,
Stanza VII

I do want to get rich but I never want to do what there is to do to get rich.

How to Write

Gertrude Stein

The first problem for all of us, men and women, is not to learn, but to unlearn.

The Washington Post

Being married is like having somebody permanently in your corner. It feels limitless, not limited.

People Magazine

Without leaps of imagination, or dreaming, we lose the excitement of possibilities. Dreaming, after all, is a form of planning.

GloriaSteinem.com

No one can give us power. If we aren't part of the process of taking it, we won't be strong enough to use it.

Take This Advice by Sandra Bark

Gloria Steinem

ꕥ

Success is always something completely different to people. I feel like I've succeeded, if I'm doing something that makes me happy and I'm not lying to anybody.

Parade magazine

Kristen Stewart

ꕥ

Once you realize that you have identified a passion, invest in yourself.

The Martha Rules

Build your business success around something that you love—
something that is inherently and endlessly interesting to you.

The Martha Rules

Martha Stewart

ço

Most mothers are instinctive philosophers.

The Minister's Wooing

When you get into a tight place and it seems you can't go on,
hold on, for that's just the place and the time that the tide will
turn.

Old Town Folks

Harriet Beecher Stowe

ço

Real love moves freely in both directions. Don't waste your
time on anything else.

Tiny Beautiful Things

You will learn a lot about yourself if you stretch in the
direction of goodness, of bigness, of kindness, of forgiveness,
of emotional bravery. Be a warrior for love.

Tiny Beautiful Things

We are all at risk of something. Of ending up exactly where we
begin, of failing to imagine and find and know and actualize who
we could be. The only difference is the distance of the leap.

O, The Oprah Magazine

Cheryl Strayed

Put binders on to those things that conspire to hold you back, especially the ones in your own head.

Success by Jena Pincott

Don't waste so much time worrying about your skin or your weight. Develop what you do, what you put your hands on in the world.

Indiana University interview

Meryl Streep

ॐ

Men are allowed to have passion and commitment for their work . . . a woman is allowed that feeling for a man, but not her work.

People magazine

Everyone has a right to love and be loved, and nobody on this earth has the right to tell anyone that their love for another human being is morally wrong.

The Advocate

I am also very proud to be a liberal. Why is that so terrible these days? The liberals were liberators—they fought slavery, fought for women to have the right to vote, fought against Hitler, Stalin, fought to end segregation, fought to end apartheid. Liberals put an end to child labor and they gave us the five day work week! What's to be ashamed of?

Harvard speech

Barbra Streisand

We need to embrace mentoring. I would encourage successful women from all walks of life to give of their valuable time to organizations that provide Canadian girls and young women with access to the life-changing benefits of mentorship.

Toronto Star

Belinda Stronach

☙

Children require guidance and sympathy far more than instruction.

Find Your Strongest Life

People seldom see the halting and painful steps by which the most insignificant success is achieved.

Letter, Oct. 30, 1887

Anne Sullivan

☙

To love is to receive a glimpse of heaven.

KarenSunde.com

Karen Sunde

☙

Love from one being to another can only be that two solitudes comes nearer, recognize and protect and comfort each other.

A Many Splendored Thing

Han Suyin (Elizabeth Comber)

As long as we dare to dream and don't get in the way of ourselves, anything is possible—there's truly no end to where our dreams can take us.

Words That Matter by editors of O, the Oprah Magazine

Hilary Swank

ᦕ

To love deeply in one direction makes us more loving in all others.

The Writings of Madame Swetchine

We are rich only through what we give, and poor only through what we refuse.

The Writings of Madame Swetchine

Sophie Swetchine

ᦕ

I realized that if you're lucky enough to be different, don't change.

Seventeen magazine

Never believe anyone who says you don't deserve what you want.

The Biography Channel

Taylor Swift

ᦕ

We need time to dream, time to remember, and time to reach the infinite. Time to be.

Parish Nursing by Solari-Twadell and McDermott

Gladys Taber

Disappointment to a noble soul is what cold water is to burning metal; it strengthens, tempers, intensifies, but never destroys it.

St. Olave's

Eliza Tabor

☙

I adore wearing gems, but not because they are mine. You can't possess radiance, you can only admire it.

My Love Affair with Jewelry

Elizabeth Taylor

☙

Thoughts are energy, and you can make your world or break your world by your thinking.

Essence Magazine

Susan L. Taylor

☙

I make the most of all that comes and the least of all that goes.

The Philosopher

Sara Teasdale

☙

Joy is a net of love by which you can catch souls.

Unbinding Your Soul

We can do no great things, only small things with great love.

Mother Teresa's Wisdom by Carol J. Mulvihill

Loneliness and feeling of being unwanted is the most terrible poverty.

Living a Connected Life

Kind words can be short and easy to speak, but their echoes are truly endless.

Truth and Dare

Smile at each other, smile at your wife, smile at your husband, smile at your children, smile at each other—it doesn't matter who it is—and that will help you to grow up in greater love for each other.

One Life to Give

Mother Teresa

❧

Once you've been in space, you appreciate how small and fragile the Earth is.

Interview by Daisaku Ikeda

Valentina Tereshkova

❧

Art is the only way to run away without leaving home.

The Creative Habit

Twyla Tharp

❧

You may have to fight a battle more than once to win it.

Deseret News

Being powerful is like being a lady. If you have to tell people you are, you aren't.

U. S. News and World Report

In politics, if you want anything said, ask a man, if you want anything done, ask a woman.

Speech at Royal Albert Hall

Margaret Thatcher

ھ

It's never too late—in fiction or in life—to revise.

NancyThayer.com

Nancy Thayer

ھ

I've always been comfortable with my sexuality. I'm blessed to have been raised by a woman who never made me feel ashamed about what's underneath my clothes. That's a part of me and I don't run away from it.

Glamour magazine

Charlize Theron

ھ

It is easier to avoid the effects of others' negativity when we question if an action or attitude is appropriately directed at us. If it isn't, we can choose to sidestep it and let it pass.

The Woman's Book of Courage

Sue Patton Thoele

If you trust your nerve as well as your skill, you're capable of a lot more than you can imagine.

Time magazine

Debi Thomas

ॐ

My father said there were two kinds of people in the world: givers and takers. The takers may eat better, but the givers sleep better.

Coach Wooden by Pat Williams and James Denney

One of the things about equality is not just that you be treated equally to a man, but that you treat yourself equally to the way you treat a man.

The Phantom Spouse by Denise V. Lang

Marlo Thomas

ॐ

Only when we are no longer afraid do we begin to live.

The Biography Channel

Courage, it would seem, is nothing less than the power to overcome danger, misfortune, fear, injustice, while continuing to affirm inwardly that life with all its sorrows and good is meaningful even if in a sense beyond our understanding, and that there is always tomorrow.

The Courage to be Happy

Dorothy Thompson

I've learned that every working mom is a superwoman.

Parade magazine

And also I think particularly as a female, you're taught to be defensive your whole life. You're taught not to be aggressive.

Interview by Jeff Otto

Uma Thurman

ଙ୍

The only way to grow is to challenge yourself.

Interview by Lance Carter

Don't let anyone, or any rejection, keep you from what you want.

Ashley Tisdale by Grace Norwich

Ashley Tisdale

ଙ୍

The best mind-altering drug is truth.

Healing Words for the Body, Mind and Spirit

The trouble with being in the rat race is that even if you win, you're still a rat.

People magazine

Lily Tomlin

ଙ୍

When people don't have an objective there's much less dynamic effort and that makes life a lot less interesting.

A World of Ideas
by Bill Moyers and Betty Flowers

Barbara Tuchman

You know, as any parent will say, you know life happens. Do the best you can. You work—it's a day at a time process. I have an unending desire to be better and make myself a better person.

Larry King Live

Tanya Tucker

❧

Yoga is so universal in its principles and so holistically beneficial, it is possible for any person, young or old, religious or agnostic, to embrace and enjoy a practice.

Living Yoga

Christy Turlington

❧

Sometimes you have to let everything go—purge yourself. If you are unhappy with anything—whatever is bringing you down—get rid of it. Because you will find that when you are free, your true creativity, your true self comes out.

I, Tina

Tina Turner

❧

People always call it luck when you've acted more sensibly than they have.

Celestial Navigation

Anne Tyler

❧

I will die for my right to be human—just human.

I Dream a World by Brian Lanker

Challenges make you discover things about yourself that you never really knew. They're what make the instrument stretch— what make you go beyond the norm.

Reader's Digest magazine

I say that if each person in this world will simply take a small piece of this huge thing, this tablecloth, bedspread, whatever, and work it regardless of the color of the yarn, we will have harmony on this planet.

Write Idea! by Elaine Mei Aoki

Cicely Tyson

&

If only we could all accept that there is no difference between us where human values are concerned. Whatever sex.

Adult Development Through Relationships,
by Vivian Rogers and David Plath

Liv Ullmann

&

Every day is a new day, and you'll never be able to find happiness if you don't move on.

Cosmopolitan magazine

Carrie Underwood

&

People who fight with fire usually end up with ashes.

Dear Abby

Abigail Van Buren

Breathing deeply and releasing fear will help you get to where you want to be.

Living Through the Meantime

When we have peace in our hearts and minds, we draw peace into our lives.

Acts of Faith

If you're not willing to let your partner see your cellulite or know your biggest fears, then you aren't really ready to share yourself.

Essence magazine

When you stand and share your story in an empowering way, your story will heal you and your story will heal somebody else.

O, The Oprah Magazine

Iyanla Vanzant

ᕲ

Optimism depends on seeing the self as full of the emotional stuff it takes to rise to the challenge and weather life's storms. Optimists believe that they are robust, and this perspective in turn allows them to choose to see the glass as half full rather than half empty.

Half Empty, Half Full

Susan C. Vaughan

ᕲ

When we take revenge against another, we lose some of our innocence.

Revenge and Forgiveness

Patrice Redd Vecchione

Women's bodies have near-perfect knowledge of childbirth. It's when their brains get involved that things can go wrong.

Baby Catcher

Peggy Vincent

ᖺ

Believing in fate has probably always arisen in part because of the delights and terrors of storytelling. We have to realize—to learn—that in life we are not the readers but the authors of our own narratives.

Beyond Fate

Margaret Visser

ᖺ

Everything about my life seemed so perfect to people. But I struggle like everyone else.

People magazine

Lindsey Vonn

ᖺ

The only real elegance is in the mind; if you've got that, the rest really comes from it.

Marie Claire magazine

Diana Vreelan

ᖺ

You can't give people pride, but you can provide the kind of understanding that makes people look to their inner strengths and find their own sense of pride.

Reader's Digest magazine

Charleszetta Waddles

Expect nothing. Live frugally on surprise.

Everyday Use

It's so clear that you have to cherish everyone.

I Dream a World by Brian Lanker

Alice Walker

༺

Most important thing in life . . . is learning how to fail.

Half Broke Horses

Life is a drama full of tragedy and comedy. You should learn to enjoy the comic episodes a little more.

The Glass Castle

Jeanette Walls

༺

Most of us have trouble juggling. The woman who says she doesn't is someone whom I admire but have never met.

The Successful Woman by Joy Brothers

To feel valued, to know, even if only once in a while, that you can do a job well is an absolutely marvelous feeling.

New Woman magazine

Success can make you go one of two ways. It can make you a prima donna, or it can smooth the edges, take away the insecurities, let the nice things come out.

Newsweek magazine

Barbara Walters

What you can't pay back you pay forward.

Farthing

If you love books enough, books will love you back.

Among Others

Jo Walton

❧

Stop playing safe.

Stop Playing Safe

Margie Warrell

❧

There is nobody in this country who got rich on his own.

CBS News

Elizabeth Warren

❧

Your life is your story, and the adventure ahead of you is the journey to fulfill your own purpose and potential.

O, The Oprah Magazine

Kerry Washington

❧

I came to understand that it was important to me to pursue those things that I cared about, and I really didn't care if people didn't like me for it.

I Dream a World by Brian Lanker

Maxine Waters

All negativity is an illusion created by the limited mind to protect and defend itself.

Chakras and Their Archetypes

Ambika Wauters

❧

There are a million ways to lose someone you love.

Good For You

Tammara Webber

❧

If we go into ourselves we find that we possess exactly what we desire.

Gravity and Grace

There is one, and only one, thing in modern society more hideous than crime—namely, repressive justice.

Human Personally

Simone Weil

❧

Real giving is when we give to our spouses what's important to them, whether we understand it, like it, agree with it, or not.

The Divorce Remedy

Michele Weiner-Davis

The word yoga comes from Sanskrit, the language of ancient India. It means union, integration, or wholeness. It is an approach to health that promotes the harmonious collaboration of the human being's three components; body, mind, spirit.

Yoga

Stella Weller

ও

Of two evils choose the prettier.

Critrion

Carolyn Wells

ও

Learn the wisdom of compromise, for it is better to bend a little than to break.

Marriage Advice

Jane Wells

ও

All serious daring starts within.

One Writer's Beginnings

Through travel I first became aware of the outside world; it was through travel that I found my own introspective way into becoming part of it.

On Writing

Eudora Welty

In most cases, suicide is a solitary event and yet it has often far-reaching repercussions for many others. It is rather like throwing a stone into a pond, the ripples spread and spread.

A Special Star

Alison Wertheimer

ಌ

You only live once, but if you do it right, once is enough.

Chicago Tribune

When I'm good I'm very, very good, but when I'm bad I'm better.

I'm No Angel

Marriage is like a book. The whole story takes place between the covers.

Sextette

Mae West

ಌ

It is always one's virtues and not one's vices that precipitate one into disaster.

The Harsh Voice

When anything important has to be written . . . I think your hand concentrates for you.

The Paris Review

You must always believe that life is as extraordinary as music says it is.

The Fountain Overflows

Rebecca West

If only we'd stop trying to be happy we could have a pretty good time.

The Hermit and the Wild Woman and Other Stories

There are two ways of spreading light: to be the candle or the mirror that reflects it.

Exploring Candle Magic by Patricia Telesco

Edith Wharton

ക

You don't luck into integrity. You work at it.

If You Ask Me

Friendship takes time and energy if it's going to work. You can luck into something great, but it doesn't last if you don't give it proper appreciation. Friendship can be so comfortable, but nurture it-don't take it for granted.

If You Ask Me

Betty White

ക

I didn't spend a lot of time thinking about as a woman how I would manage differently—I was just happy to be managing.

Forbes magazine

Margaret "Meg" Whitman

ക

Whatever women do they must do twice as well as men to be thought half as good. Luckily, this is not difficult.

Canada Month magazine

Charlotte Whitton

It is essential to our well-being, and to our lives, that we play and enjoy life. Every single day, do something that makes your heart sing.

Making Your Dreams Come True

Marcia Wieder

ꝏ

May there always be a little faith in your doubt.

The Song of the Seed

It is risky to trust. I may give someone my heart, and they may leave town with it.

The Song of the Seed

Macrina Wiederkehr

ꝏ

Don't become something just because someone else wants you to, or because it's easy; you won't be happy. You have to do what you really, really, really, really want to do, even if it scares the shit out of you.

Elle magazine

Kristen Wiig

ꝏ

Love lights more fires than hate extinguishes.

Optimism

Life is a garden forever in flower.

Entre-Acte Reveries

All the past is not worth one today.

New Year

Ella Wheeler Wilcox

✍

Remember well, and bear in mind, a constant friend is hard to find.

Laura Ingalls Wilder, Farm Journalist,
by Stephen Hines

I am beginning to learn that it is the sweet, simple things of life which are the real ones after all.

Laura Ingalls Wilder, Farm Journalist,
by Stephen Hines

A good laugh overcomes difficulties and dissipates more dark clouds than any one thing.

Writings to Young Women

Laura Ingalls Wilder

✍

The difficulty of retirement planning is its parameters—an undermined amount of money, to last an unknown length of time, in a highly volatile financial environment including fluctuations in the stock market, the cost of living, medical care, taxes, and Social Security.

All About Retirement Funds

Ellie Williams

Tennis is just a game. Family is forever.

On the Line

Serena Williams

ॐ

Joy is what happens when we allow ourselves to recognize how good things really are.

Woman's Worth

Practice of forgiveness is our most important contribution to the healing of the world.

A Return to Love

A person acting from a motivation of contribution and service rises at such a level of moral authority, that worldly success is a natural result.

A Return to Love

There is a plan for each of us, and each of us is precious. As we open our hearts more and more, we're moved in the directions in which we're supposed to go.

A Return to Love

Marianne Williamson

ॐ

My deepest impulses are optimistic; an attitude that seems to me as spiritually necessary and proper as it is intellectually suspect.

Beginning to See the Light

Ellen Willis

Luck is a matter of preparation meeting opportunity.

O, The Oprah Magazine

Forget about the fast lane. If you really want to fly, just harness your power to your passion.

Forbes magazine

Be thankful for what you have; you'll end up having more. If you concentrate on what you don't have, you will never, ever have enough.

The Authentic Career

It isn't until you come to a spiritual understanding of who you are—not necessarily a religious feeling, but deep down, the spirit within—that you begin to take control.

Everybody Loves Oprah! by Norman King

I've come to believe that each of us has a personal calling that's as unique as a fingerprint—and that the best way to succeed is to discover what you love and then find a way to offer it to others in the form of service, working hard, and also allowing the energy of the universe to lead you.

O, The Oprah Magazine

Oprah Winfrey

൙

If you make fun of bad persons you make yourself beneath them.

Life Among the Plutes

Sarah Winnemucca

What you risk reveals what you value.

Written on the Body

Love is an experiment . . . what happens next is always surprising.

The Stone Gods

When I fell in love it was as though I looked into a mirror for the first time and saw myself.

Postmodern Studies,
by Helena Grace and Tim Woods

The Buddhists say there are 149 ways to god. I'm not looking for god, only for myself, and that is far more complicated.

Sexing the Cherry

Jeanette Winterson

༥

I think women are natural caretakers. We take care of everybody—our husbands and our kids and our dogs—and don't spend a lot of time just getting back and taking time out.

Working Woman magazine

And I want to say that my grandmother was one of the biggest inspirations in my life. She taught me how to be a real woman, to have strength and self-respect, and to never give those things away.

Academy Award acceptance speech

Reese Witherspoon

My parents always allowed me to fail when I was growing up, and I think that gave me a lot of strength going forward in my life. I lost high-school and junior-high elections when I ran for class president. I learned early in life to get up and dust yourself off and keep going.

Newsweek magazine

Andrea Wong

ᔓ

Love had a thousand shapes.

To the Lighthouse

As a woman I have no country. As a woman I want no country. As a woman, my country is the whole world.

Three Guineas

Women have served all the centuries as looking glasses possessing the magic and delicious power of reflecting the figure of man at twice its natural size.

A Room of One's Own

Virginia Woolf

ᔓ

Marriage is to family what legs are to a table.

Family: An Exploration

Betty Jane Wylie

Men are taught to apologize for their weaknesses, women for their strengths.

The Power of Women,
by Susan Nolen-Hoeksema

Lois Wyse

༁

We cannot expect in the immediate future that all women who seek it will achieve full equality of opportunity. But if women are to start moving towards that goal, we must match our aspirations with the competence, courage and determination to succeed.

Nobel Prize banquet speech

Roslyn Sussman Yalow

༁

Be pretty if you can, be witty if you must, but be gracious if it kills you.

A Swarm of Wasps by Patricia Falk Feeley

I've had a lot of opportunities in my life . . . I don't feel that I've faced discrimination. I've had every chance to succeed and more, and I think that's what all women should have.

Reuters

Janet Yellen

༁

You can't win them all—but you can try.

How to Be Like Women Athletes of Influence,
by Pat Williams

The formula for success is simple: practice and concentration, then more practice and more concentration.

Soul Beautiful, Naturally by Leanna Burns

Babe Didrikson Zaharias

&

Courage is simply fear that has said its prayers!

Addicted

Zane

&

Because if you love someone, you love them all the way. You love them even when they make mistakes.

In the Age of Love and Chocolate

Gabrielle Zevin

List of Authors Quoted

Jane Ace
Abigail Adams
Jane Addams
Freda Adler
Christina Aguilera
Anouk Aimee
Jessica Alba
Madeleine Albright
Louisa May Alcott
Margaret Walker Alexander
Lily Allen
Susanne Alleyn
Joan Wester Anderson
Marian Anderson
Pamela Anderson
Maya Angelou
Jennifer Aniston
Susan B. Anthony
Corazon Aquino
Diane Arbus
Mary Kay Ash
Nancy Astor
Amelia Atwater-Rhodes
Margaret Atwood
Jane Austen

Lauren Bacall
Michelle Bachelet
Joan Baez
Pearl Bailey
Tammy Baldwin
Lucille Ball
Tyra Banks
Brigitte Bardot
Myrtie Barker

Roseanne Barr
Mary Barra
Rona Barrett
Ethel Barrymore
Anne L. Barstow
Ardelia Cotton Barton
Clara Barton
Vicki Baum
Ann Baxter
Melody Beattie
Simone de Beauvoir
Martha Beck
Pat Benatar
Ingrid Bengis
Margot Bennett
Gail Rubin Bereny
Candice Bergen
Ingrid Bergman
Laura Berman
Sandra Bernhardt
Mary Frances Berry
Murray Bethel
Beyonce (Knowles)
Jacqeline Bisset
Antoinette Brown Blackwell
Amy Bloom
Sarah Knowles Bolton
Erma Bombeck
Corrie Boom
Elayne Boosler
Joan Borysenko
Margaret Bourke-White
Elizabeth Bowen
Barbara Boxer
Marion Zimmer Bradley

Anne Bradstreet
Angela Braly
Sarah Ban Breathnach
Kathleen A. Brehony
Fannie Brice
Patricia Briggs
Christie Brinkley
Charlotte Bronte
Emily Bronte
Anita Brookner
Gwendolyn Brooks
Joyce Brothers
Brene Brown
Helen Gurley Brown
Rita Mae Brown
Elizabeth Barrett Browning
Quentin Bryce
Pearl Buck
Sandra Bullock
Charlotte Bunch
Margaret A. Burkhardt
Carol Burnett
Ursula Burns
Ellen Burstyn
Barbara Bush
Candace Bushnell

Helen Caldicott
Maria Callas
Julia Cameron
Jacqueline Carey
Julia Carney
Rachel Carson
Catherine. Duchess of Cambridge
Carrie Chapman Catt
Margaret Chan
Gabrielle "Coco" Chanel
Chris Chase
Julia Child
Laura Chinchilla

Margaret Cho
Rea Dawn Chong
Shirley Chisholm
Kate Chopin
Agatha Christie
Ciara (Ciara Princess Harris)
Cassandra Clare
Anita H. Clayton
Connie Clerici
Hillary Rodham Clinton
Alexandra Pauline "Sasha" Cohen
Arianne Cohen
Johnnetta Betsch Cole
Joanna Coles
Sidonie Gabrielle Colette
Toni Collette
Judy Collins
Suzanne Collins
Nadia Comaneci
Ivy Compton-Burnett
Eliza Cook
Kelly Corrigan
Katie Couric
Cindy Crawford
Sheryl Crow
Mary Crowley
Marie Curie
A.B. Curtiss
Miley Cyrus

Bette Davis
Barbara De Angelis
Ruby Dee
Ellen DeGeneres
Michelle Delio
Margo Demello
Sarah Dessen
Gail Devers
Diana, Princess of Wales
Emily Dickinson

Joan Didion
Marlene Dietrich
Annie Dillard
Phyllis Diller
Dorothy Dix
Rita Dove
Maureen Dowd
Stephanie Dowrick
Margaret Drabble
Hilary Duff
Isadora Duncan
Dianne M. Durkin
Andrea Dworkin

Amelia Earhart
Crystal Eastman
Isabelle Eberhardt
Mary Baker Eddy
Marian Wright Edelman
Gertrude Ederle
Maria Edgeworth
Barbara Ehrenreich
Carmen Electra
George Eliot (Mary Evans)
Elizabeth II
Linda Ellerbee
Nora Ephron
Louise Erdrich
Laura Esquivel
Gloria Estefan
Melissa Etheridge

Florence Falk
Donna Farhi
Wendy Farley
Kathy Farrell-Kingsley
Dianne Feinstein
Edna Ferber
Fergie (Fergie Duhamel)
Tina Fey

Jonna Field
Karen Finerman
Mary Jane Finsand
Carrie Fisher
M. F. K. Fisher
Ella Fitzgerald
Penelope Fitzgerald
Peggy Fleming
D. C. Fontana
Margot Fonteyn
Betty Ford
Dian Fossey
Megan Fox
Arlene Francis
Anne Frank
Missy Franklin
Rosaland Franklin
Pauline Frederick
Barbara L. Fredrickson
Marilyn French
Dorothy Fuldheim
Margaret Fuller

Eva Gabor
Zsa Zsa Gabor
Lady Gaga
Indira Gandhi
Sonia Gandhi
Greta Garbo
Lisa Gardner
Melinda Gates
Park Geun-hye
Miep Gies
Elizabeth Gilbert
Anne Gilchrist
Ellen Gilchrist
Julia Gillard
Ruth Bader Ginsburg
Nikki Giovanni
Lillian Gish

Ellen Glasgow
Susan Glaspell
Gail Godwin
Jane G. Goldberg
Emma Goldman
Jane Goodall
Linda Goodman
Nadine Gordimer
Ruth Gordo
Barbara Gordon
Annie Gottlieb
Katherine Graham
Martha Graham
Lee Grant
Francine du Plessix Gray
Germaine Greer
Judith Guest

Rae Hachton
Sarah Josepha Hale
Joan Halifax
Judy Hall
Diane F. Halpern
Margaret Halsey
Laurell K. Hamilton
Sheenah Hankin
Lorraine Hansberry
Angie Harmon
Frances Harper
Joanne Harris
Patricia Roberts Harris
Josephine Hart
Louise Hart
Anne Hathaway
Goldie Hawn
Louise L. Hay
Helen Hayes
Carolyn Heilbrun
Lillian Hellman
Leona Helmsley

Mariel Hemingway
Amy Hempel
Patti Callahan Henry
Audrey Hepburn
Katharine Hepburn
Anita Hill
Raicho Hiratsuka
Jane Hirshfield
Shere Hite
Martha Lavinia Hoffman
Hilary Hoge
E. E. Holmes
Lori Hope
Grace Hopper
Lena Horne
Jane Howard
Julia Ward Howe
Ethel Puffer Howes
Susan Hubbard
Vanessa Hudgens
Kate Hudson
Arianna Huffington
Margaret Wolfe Hungerford
Charlayne Hunter-Gault
Fannie Hurst
Zora Neale Hurston

India.Arie (India Arie Simpson)
Janey Ironside

Glenda Jackson
Mahalia Jackson
E. L. James
Jenna Jameson
Elizabeth Janeway
Susan J. Jeffers
Elfriede Jelinek
Mae C. Jemison
Valerie Jeremijenko
Scarlett Johansson

Barbara Johnson
Carrie Johnson
Dorothea Johnson
Heidi Johnson
Angelina Jolie
Allison Jones
Erica Jong
Jeanette de Jonk
Janis Joplin
Barbara Jordon
Florence Griffith Joyner
Jackie Joyner-Kersee
Naomi Judd
Andrea Jung

Gigi Kaeser
Frido Kahlo
Rosabeth Moss Kanter
Donna Karan
Ruth Mazo Karras
Deena Kastor
Hellen Keller
Fanny Kemble
Sally Kempton
Katrina Kenison
Caroline Kennedy
Florynce R. Kennedy
Eileen Kennedy-Moore
Corita Kent
Sherrilyn Kenyon and Dianna Love
Deborah Kerr
Kersha (Bailey)
Ellen Key
Sue Monk Kidd
Nicole Kidman
Nell Kimball
Emily Kimbrough
Billie Jean King
Gayle King
Daphne Rose Kingma

Barbara Kingsolver
Maxine Hong Kingston
Kimberly Kirberger
Christina Fernandez de Kirchner
Anne Klein
Melanie Klein
Lisa Kleypas
Amy Klobuchar
Mirra Komarovsky
Cheris Kramerae
Elizabeth Kubler-Ross
Maggie Kuhn
Chandrika Kumaratunga
Michelle Kwan

Christine Lagarde
Caroline Lalive
Anne Lamott
Ann Landers (Eppie Lederer)
Mary L. Landrieu
Dorothea Lange
Loretta LaRoche
Estee Lauder
Avril Lavigne
Mary Leakey
Fran Lebowitz
Harper Lee
Jennette Lee
Tanith Lee
Ursula K. Le Guin
Harriet Lerner
Rokelle Lerner
Elizabeth Lesser
Doris Lessing
Gail Carson Levine
Susan Lieberman
Dana Lightman
Anne Morrow Lindbergh
Eva Longoria
Jennifer Lopez

Sophia Loren
Courtney Love
Patricia Love
Carey Lowell
Clare Boothe Luce
Joan Lunden

Gloria Macapagal-Arroyo
Rose Macaulay
Lucy MacDonald
Lesley Mackley
Shirley MacLaine
Rachel Maddow
Madonna
Katherine Mansfield
Hilary Mantel
Gina Maranto
Elisabeth Marbury
Beryl Markham
Stephanie Marston
Jean Marzollo
Mary Matalin
Joanne Mattern
Marissa Mayer
Clara McBride-Hale
Megan McCafferty
Anne McCaffrey
Mary McCarthy
Barbara McClintock
Mignon McLaughlin
Terry McMillan
Margaret Mead
Golda Meir
Lise Meitner
Angela Merkel
Bette Midler
Barbara A. Mikulski
Edna St. Vincent Millay
Karen Maezen Miller
Kate Millet

Liza Minnelli
Joni Mitchell
Margaret Mitchell
Anne Shannon Monroe
Marilyn Monroe
Maria Montessori
Lucy Maud Montgomery
Demi Moore
Marianne Moore
Susanna Moore
Jeanne Moreau
Dorothy Morrison
Toni Morrison
Doris Mortman
Constance Baker Motley
Ethel Watts Mumford
Alice Munro
Catherine Gilbert Murdock
Iris Murdoch
Anne Murray
Judy Murray
Patty Murray
Caroline Myss

Linda Naiman
Ivy Naistadt
Martina Navratilova
Marianne E. Neifert
Louise Nevelson
Anais Nin
Alyson Noel
Indra Krishnamurthy Nooyi
Marsha Norman
Kathleen Norris
Christiane Northrup

Michelle Obama
Sandra Day O'Conner
Mary O'Hara
Georgia O'Keeffe

Jackie Kennedy Onassis
Barbara O'Neal
Suze Orman

Amanda Palmer
Barbara Park
Dorothy Parker
Sarah Jessica Parker
Rosa Parks
Leslie L. Parrott
Dolly Parton
Ann Patchett
Praatibha Patil
Alice Paul
Anna Palova
Judith Peacock
Nancy Pelosi
Alexandra Penney
Frances Perkins
Eva Peron
Katy Perry
Mary Pickford
Marge Piercy
Sylvia Plath
Barbara Pletcher
Letty Cottin Pogrebin
Katha Pollitt
Eleanor H. Porter
Katherine Anne Porter
Emily Post
Eleanor Powell
Georgia Davis Powers
Sephanie Powers
Leontyne Price
Cherie Priest
Ivy Baker Priest
E. Annie Proulx

Mary Quant
Anna Quindlen

Mary Anne Radmacher
Alice Radosh
Ayn Rand
Lisa Randall
Nancy Rathburn
Rachel Ray
Pauline Reage (Dominique Aury)
Vanessa Redgrave
Tracy Redies
Agnes Repplier
Yasmina Reza
Anne Rice
Adrienne Rich
Sally Ride
Amanda Robb
Julia Roberts
Nora Roberts
Robin Roberts
Mary Robinson
Rachel Robinson
Anita Roddick
Ginger Rogers
Virginia "Ginni" Rometty
Eleanor Roosevelt
Irene Rosenfeld
JoAnn Ross
Geneen Roth
Dilma Rousseff
Helen Rowland
J. K. Rowling
Rachel Roy
Wilma Rudolph
Jane Rule
Dora Russell
Rosalind Russell
Meg Ryan

Guler Sabanci
Vita Sackville-West
Ruth St. Denis

George Sand (Amantine Lucile
Aurore Dupin)
Sheryl Sandberg
Margaret Sanger
May Sarton
Diane Sawyer
Dorothy Sayers
Pepper Schwartz
Gloria Dean Randle Scott
Kyra Sedgwick
Anna Sewell
Jane Seymour
Betty Shabazz
Jeanne Shaheen
Shakira
Sheila A. Sharpe
Salley E. Shaywitz
Gail Sheehy
Mary Wollstonecraft Shelley
Karen Sheriff
Mikaela Shiffrin
Marci Shimoff
Dinah Shore
Maria Shriver
Simone Signoret
Beverly Sills
Ellen Johnson Sirleaf
Anna Deavere Smith
Jada Pinkett Smith
Patti Smith
Ann Snitow
Rebecca Solnit
Susan Sontag
Sonia Sotomayor
Muriel Spark
Britney Spears
Madame de Stael
Elizabeth Cady Stanton
Gertrude Stein
Gloria Steinem

Kristen Stewart
Martha Stewart
Harriet Beecher Stowe
Cheryl Strayed
Meryl Streep
Barbra Streisand
Belinda Stronach
Anne Sullivan
Karen Sunde
Han Suyin (Elizabeth Comber)
Hilary Swank
Sophie Swetchine
Taylor Swift

Cladys Taber
Eliza Tabor
Elizabeth Taylor
Susan L. Taylor
Sara Teasdale
Mother Teresa
Valentina Tereshkova
Twyla Tharp
Margaret Thatcher
Nancy Thayer
Charlize Theron
Sue Patton Thoele
Debi Thomas
Marlo Thomas
Dorothy Thompson
Uma Thurman
Ashley Tisdale
Lily Tomlin
Barbara Tuchman
Tanya Tucker
Christy Turlington
Tina Turner
Anne Tyler
Cicely Tyson

Liv Ulmann

Carrie Underwood

Abigail Van Buren
Iyanla Vanzant
Susan C. Vaughan
Patrice Redd Vecchione
Peggy Vincent
Margaret Visser
Lindsey Vonn
Diana Vreelan

Charleszetta Waddles
Alice Walker
Jeanette Walls
Barbara Walters
Jo Walton
Margie Warrell
Elizabeth Warren
Kerry Washington
Maxine Waters
Ambika Wauters
Tammara Webber
Simone Weil
Michele Weiner-Davis
Stella Weller
Carolyn Wells
Jane Wells
Eudora Welty
Alison Wertheimer

Mae West
Rebecca West
Edith Wharton
Betty White
Margaret "Meg" Whitman
Charlotte Whitton
Marcia Wieder
Macrina Wiederkehr
Kristen Wiig
Ella Wheeler Wilcox
Laura Ingalls Wilder
Ellie Williams
Serena Williams
Marianne Williamson
Ellen Willis
Oprah Winfrey
Sarah Winnemucca
Jeanette Winterson
Reese Witherspoon
Andrea Wong
Virginia Woolf
Betty Jane Wylie
Lois Wyse
Roslyn Sussman Yalow
Janet Yellen

Babe Didrikson Zaharias
Zane
Gabrielle Zevin

Acknowledgments

We want to personally thank all of the fabulous women in our lives: girlfriends, mothers, sisters, and you. Most important to acknowledge is the unconditional love and support of our mothers: Phyllis Levin, Fran Lalive, and Kathy Northcutt, and our sisters: Wendy Levin Shaw, Isabelle Lalive, and Kelly Northcutt. Without you, there would not be an Inspired Life Network. You are our original network and we thank you from the bottom of our hearts.

We would also like to thank those who helped make this book a reality. Publishing executive Rick Frishman is the founder of the seminar Author101University.com. During one of Rick's seminars, we met Bill Gladstone, founder and president of Waterside Productions. Bill embraced the concept of Inspired Life Network as a way to help people, especially women. He introduced us to SelectBooks' president Kenzi Sugihara. Kenzi encouraged and supported us through the entire publishing process.

Additionally we are grateful to family and friends who helped with quotations research and verification, including Jill Wichner, Krystle Worster, Andrew J. Brown, Ben Louis Shaw, and Daniel and Shayna Shaw, Jackie Kuusinen, Robin Schepper, and Nancy Sugihara.

And finally without our loving support group, none of this is possible. Thank you to Jules Meeker, Kelly Proudly, Paige Boucher, Erin Brosterhous, Daria Anti, Nelson Carmichael, Scott Nielson, and June Wolff.

About the Authors

Caroline Lalive Carmichael, a two-time Olympian (Nagano 1998 and Salt Lake City 2002) and three-time United States National Alpine Skiing Champion, spent thirteen years on the U.S. Ski team. Caroline presently works as a television sports commentator (NBC, Fox Sports, Versus, and ESPN), philanthropist, model, and ski coach. Caroline has had the privilege of working with Armed Forces Entertainment. She has visited military troops around the world. Caroline was part of the 2013 Winter Sports Tour with the State Department in Kyrgyzstan.

She knows how goal setting, hard work, perseverance, dedication, and the support of community can lead to success and fulfillment. Articulate, passionate, and funny, Caroline has the compassion, confidence, and skills to inspire others and share her life experience beyond the ski slope. She hosts each seminar, adds her insights, and facilitates a unique Inspired Life Network experience.

Sarah Coleman grew up in Steamboat Springs, Colorado, and is a longtime friend of Caroline's. She has always enjoyed an outdoor lifestyle and many sports from skiing to biking. Sarah graduated cum laude from the University of San Diego with a degree in communications with a media emphasis. Sarah holds a personal training license from ACE, the American Counsel on Exercise, and multiple CrossFit certifications.

Self-motivated Sarah started two companies dedicated to living healthy lifestyles: A Weight Lifted Fitness Camp and Food To Fit nutrition packages. Sarah understands that to live a balanced and inspired life, one must start with the basics of healthy fitness and nutritional habits. She is the business manager for Inspired Life Network and a creative force behind the team.

Howard Alan Levin (Hal), an entrepreneur, certified professional spiritual healer, and author, has a vision. His previous books are *Quotations for Successful Living*, *Letters to an Angel*, and *A History of Horses Told by Horses*. Hal attended the University of Copenhagen in Denmark and graduated from Oneonta State University of New York with a BA in business and economics.

Having visited more than forty countries, Hal has met women all over the world, from impoverished mothers to world leaders. He's seen gender inequality in nearly all societies and populations and recognizes the urgent need for more female leaders. He believes women serving as mentors and role models are needed to bring our world into better balance. It's a tall order, but Hal wants to do what he can to evoke that change, and he believes that his friends, Caroline and Sarah, have what it takes to light the spark in others.

Caroline, Sarah and Hal are the managing directors of Inspired Life Network. The Inspired Life Network can be described as a journey, a mindset, and a community—all designed to inspire and empower women everywhere to connect with their unique mind, body and spirit and grow into their full potential.

For more information or to share a thoughtful inspiring quote, please visit us at
www.InspiredLifeNetwork.com.